Understanding Tourism Economics

UNDERSTANDING TOURISM ECONOMICS

KUNAL CHATTOPADHYAY

KANISHKA PUBLISHERS, DISTRIBUTORS
NEW DELHI-110 002

KANISHKA PUBLISHERS, DISTRIBUTORS
4697/5-21A, Ansari Road, Daryaganj
New Delhi-110 002
Phones : 2327 0497, 2328 8285
Fax : 011-2328 8285
e-mail: kanishka_publishing@yahoo.co.in

Understanding Tourism Economics

First Published 2008

ISBN 978-81-8457-040-3

PRINTED IN INDIA

Published by Madan Sachdeva for Kanishka Publishers, Distributors, 4697/5-21A, Ansari Road, Daryaganj, New Delhi-110 002; Typeset by Sunshine Graphics, Delhi, and Printed at Nice Printing Press, Delhi.

To

Prof. Amitabha Sen
and
Prof. H. Leo Theuns

Foreword

It is a pleasure and an honour to be invited to write this foreword for Dr. Kunal Chattopadhyay's new book: *UnderstandingTourism Economics*. In this short textbook, he covers in a systematic and interesting manner a wide range of topics essential for the economics of tourism.

The book has been developed in a constructively critical manner and pays due attention to the importance of concepts and definitions. Furthermore, this book introduces some relatively advanced techniques, which can be applied to the economic analysis of tourism. However, this is done in a manner that enables their applicability to be readily appreciated by students.

An important feature of this book is that the economic analysis outlined in it is illustrated by examples and case studies. These mainly, but not exclusively, relate to India. This is no doubt a feature that will be welcomed by Indian students and their lecturers.

Dr. Kunal Chattopadhyay also introduces some relatively new topics, several of which have become of major importance in recent years. These topics include terrorism and tourism, the cost of which he illustrates by drawing on experiences in Jammu and Kashmir. He also gives attention to tourism and the environment, a subject that has been given increasing attention in recent times.

In his conclusion, Dr. Chattopadhyay briefly explores such interesting topics as medical tourism (which has grown in India, China, Thailand and elsewhere in the developing world) and he provides advice on how India can expand its inbound tourism. As he correctly points out, growth in inbound tourism to India has seriously lagged behind the growth of inbound tourism to China. Given India's natural historical and cultural attractions, India has considerable scope to boost its inbound tourism.

This textbook will provide students of tourism economics with a sound foundation for their subject. It will help foster expertise in Tourism Economics and thus contribute to tourism development in India. It deserves to be widely used as a text.

Clem Tisdell
The University of Queensland
Brisbane 4072, Australia

Preface

Over last 30 years tourism as a separate discipline has been introduced in a good number of universities and management institutes in India. Although there are few books of foreign origin in the market, they fail to meet the needs of our students for one reason or another. Unfortunately the books on tourism published locally so far have not proved very helpful either. Most of these books are either too descriptive or lack serious economic contents. More importantly the scope of getting knowledge on state of the art researches and applications of various statistical tools are seldom fulfilled in these books. Given this reality, the present work was undertaken at the request of students when I was teaching at Indian Institute of Social Welfare and Business Management, Calcutta and International Institute of Advanced Studies, Calcutta. Apart from students, my involvement with Board of Studies at Vidyasagar University in preparing vocational curriculum of Tourism induced me further to pen down the present monograph. In one sense the book is a revised version with little theoretical twist of its predecessor, *Economic Impact of Tourism Development—An Indian Experience*, which was well received.

The present book is intended to meet the need of graduate level students with training in intermediate economic theory. The overall approach remains an economic one. Mathematical requirements are kept to a minimum. Our objective is to make the vast literature accessible as much as possible and give it a well-structured treatment of the subject. It is also hoped that the book would be helpful in stimulating further research interest in the field of tourism.

There is a contention held by a group of authors that Indian researchers are compelled to their empirical work with theories developed elsewhere and often irrelevant to the Indian milieu. Furthermore, the use of mathematics stems partly from excess of theoretical abstraction. Nevertheless, the theories which developed elsewhere, as methodological tools cannot and should not be ignored.

I begin with an overview of the definitions of tourism (Chapter 2). The idea of lèisure comes as a central theme. The chapter also deals with various types of tourism. Chapter 3 shifts the focus to the economic rationalities of tourism with special emphasis on its role in regional development, international trade and human resource development. Chapter 4 reviews different statistical and mathematical techniques in determining tourist demand. The chapter therefore, takes an applied nature and inventories the most crucial empirical exercises in contemporary tourism research in various countries both developed and developing. Chapter 5 covers different impacts of tourism. In estimating both direct and indirect economic impacts application of the concept of 'economic multiplier' has been discussed here. A considerable portion of the chapter is devoted towards measuring the benefit associated with the development of tourist accommodations and attractions. Chapter 6 introduces the frontier area of environment or environmental economics. The intimate links between tourism and environment have been investigated and various estimation procedures of environmental impact assessment are also examined critically. Chapter 7 examines the nature and extent of an enigmatic and compelling phenomenon, 'terrorism' and its impact upon tourism. In the concluding chapter few observations on present Indian and Chinese tourism have been cast in the context of current global world scenario.

I am immensely grateful to Professor Clem Tisdell, Professor Emeritus, School of Economics, University of Queensland, Australia for kindly agreeing to write the foreword of this volume. My deep gratitude goes to Professor H. Leo Theuns of Tilburg University, the Netherlands. He inspired me constantly by supplying various research materials not available in India and made valuable comments on the earlier version of the book. I owe a lot to Professor Brian Archer of Department of Management Studies for Tourism and Hotel Industries, University of Surrey, U.K. He had gone through a portion of Chapter 4 and made valuable comments. I am deeply indebted to Professor Amitabha Sen of Kalyani University, who has lavished his valuable time to refurnish my aptitude and instill motivation. I also benefited much from our discussions, and from his many observations. I am thankful to Professor Jyoti Parikh of Indira Gandhi Institute of Development Research, Mumbai. She encouraged me to link environmental accounting with tourism earning. A portion of environmental impact assessment was the outcome of the two World Bank aided "India: Environmental Management Capacity Building (EMCaB) Technical Assistance" projects. I would like to thank Dr. Amitava Mitra of Arunachal University. It was a fascinating experience to work with him in one of the EMCaB Technical Assistance Projects.

In addition to the names already mentioned, there are many fine people, who helped me in ways beyond measure. The invitation of Mr. G. Malik, the former Director, Ministry of Economics and Statistics, Government of Jammu and Kashmir was one of the main spirits behind the chapter dealing with 'Tourism and Terrorism'. I owe a great deal to Dr. Chiranjib Neogi of Indian Statistical Institute, Calcutta for his wonderful ability of withstanding the trouble caused by me even in wee hours for computational advice. I must mention the name of Mr. Madan Sachdeva of Kanishka for his sincere interest to give birth of this volume. Finally, I would like to record my deep appreciation to my wife Nandini and daughters Madhuja and Adrija, who had always been the silent sentinels in defence of peace at home.

Calcutta
10 October, 2007 **Kunal Chattopadhyay**

Contents

Chapter One

Introduction

'Tourism', said Antonio Savignac, the former secretary general of the World Tourism Organization (WTO), 'will become the world's number one export industry by the turn of the 20th century.' According to the WTO's projection, money generated from the global exchange through tourism will soon exceed earnings through trade in oil, currently the world's number one export. According to US based Wharton Econometric Forecasting Associates, travel and tourism is the largest industry in the world in terms of employment. Moreover, the governments are US $166 billion richer as a result of tourism related tax revenues.

The decade of the 1960's has been described as a period of unparalleled optimism over the potential of tourism to benefit economic development. The widespread optimism of the youthful 1960's led to the theoretical justifications during the 1970's in favour of a more critical look at tourism. Development of various statistical methods and economic theories started to be tested in the problems relating to tourism. Techniques like Linear Programming, Data Envelopment Analysis, and Input-Output analysis were used in tourism research successfully. Likewise valuation of extra market commodities has opened up new vistas of environmental valuation of tourism.

Tourism is therefore, no more a sunrise industry today. Subsequently, economic consequences of tourism loomed large before the researchers, policy makers and business personnel engaged in this industry. Many developing countries are today aware of the potential benefits of tourism and most of those having suitable tourism infrastructure are well-ahead in the way of exploiting them. Scientific researches on the subject had also started to emerge in these countries, which seldom attract attention of the research communities in the developed world.

The worldwide interest in tourism research has been impressive. This development may indicate that tourism as a field of investigation is finally coming of age. There are a number of ways to gauge this popularity. Among them is increase in the number of articles, books, journals; sizable number of professors of tourism and growing number of colleges and universities with specialization in tourism studies.

In the same vein, perhaps of special interest to the scholarly community, is the growing interest of studying tourism at the doctoral level as indicated by the small but growing number of doctoral dissertations focusing on tourism. Jafari and Dean (1988) made a computer search of doctoral dissertations resulted in 157 titles with touristic focus, written between 1951-1987. It had been observed that the largest number of dissertations on tourism was in the field of economics (40), followed by anthropology (25), geography (24) and recreation (23) (Table 1.1). One can rest assured that the trend has been impressive later on.

In recent years, there has been a rethinking as to the line on which trade between LDCs and developed countries take place. In the face of current difficulties and hurdles in boosting merchandise exports, study on trade in services for developing countries is important. In view of this recent trend of the emergence

Table 1.1
Main Disciplines of Dissertation

Discipline	*Number*
Economics	40
Anthropology	25
Geography	24
Recreation	23
Business Administration	11
Education	9
Sociology	7
Urban Regional Planning	7
Political Science	5
Fine Arts	1
Social Work	1
Theology	1
History	1
Mass Communication	1
Public Relations	1
Total	*157*

and phenomenal growth of the service sectors, the emphasis was put in the first meeting of UNCTAD committee on foreign exchange earning from invisibles. In many developing countries tourism (with its typical basket of product-mix) is emerging as a quaternary sector. The most characteristic and seemingly paradoxical thing about tourism is that it essentially represents trade in non-traded goods (Sen, 1985). Nonetheless, it is a matter of surprise that tourism has for so long been completely ignored by trade theorists.

In the context of present global scenario and more importantly after the advent of Purchasing Power Parity (PPP), tourism emerged with greater strength and significance. PPP is defined as the number of units of a country's currency required to buy the same amount of goods and services in the domestic market as one dollar would buy in US. By PPP criterion, the currencies of developing countries are undervalued, not overvalued as the conventional wisdom maintains. Hence, high spending western visitors get plenty of services at less cost in countries like India and China. Measured in PPP of national currencies, the GDP of India is the sixth largest in the world and China is the third.

Divergence between market exchange rate and PPP exchange rate can arise for a variety of reasons. Presence of non-traded goods is one of them (Balassa, 1964). The relative price of non-traded goods, service in particular is lower in a poor country than in a rich one (Bhagwati, 1984). Natural resources are mostly non-traded and to a large extent low-priced in a developing economy. Hence, Foreign Direct Investment (FDI) will be attracted to the natural resource based industries in such economies (Sau, 1993). Here lie the vast prospects of tourism, particularly international tourism. This is because if capital inflow occurs for resale in domestic market then export will suffer and the very policy of opening the frontier will fail.

The growing global significance of tourism is a phenomenon recognized by the WTO with the introduction of GATS. But from the point of view of tourism and product development, globalization provides a mixed set of blessings. Globalization can provide a consistency in product standards that help to overcome the uncertainties that generally accompany travel and tourism product quality. Therefore, if a client books a hotel room in a Welcome group hotel in Goa, s/he can be confident of the parameters likely to be provided. In contrast to this aspect, globalization can result in major international companies dominating overseas market. Such events fuel antagonism. Nevertheless, one cannot ignore the fact that globalization of the world economy is a process that has been embraced by tourism which has been a pioneer in terms of both liberalization and global expansion.

Chapter Two

Definition and Types of Tourism

Definition

Tourism has its testimonies in the earliest records of history and has recorded phenomenal growth during last century. From 1980-2000, global tourism receipts increased at an annual rate of nearly 8 per cent, much faster than the rate of world economic growth of around 3 per cent. The trend is almost uninterrupted in spite of occasional down swing due to some stochastic factors like terrorism, bird flue and the like.

Different authors defined tourism differently. R. De Meyer defined tourism as, "A collective term for human movement and its attendant activities caused by exteriorization and fulfillment of the desire to escape, which is more or less latent in everybody" (Kaul, 1985). The definition seems to lack precision and is not very useful for analytical purpose. Bernecker provided a more workable definition of tourism. As per his definition, "Tourism is the sum of the relations and services connected with a temporary and voluntary change of residence for non-commercial or non-professional reasons." This implies that the change of residence of a tourist must be (*i*) voluntary, (*ii*) of a temporary nature and (*iii*) for a non-commercial or non-professional purpose.

Unlike the first definition, Bernecker's definition is precise. But it is too precise or narrow. In the first place, the distinction between what is voluntary and what is not is of one of degree rather than of kind. In a sense, all travel is voluntary since, in a modern world, only a free agent performs travel. A person kidnapped or exiled from his own country is not traveller or a tourist. On the other hand, a person seeking refuge to a neighbouring country to escapc from the clutches of law or from political persecution is also making a voluntary decision though it is the forces of circumstances which is compelling him to leave his home land for the time being. Secondly, while there could be no difference of opinion regarding change of residence, all tourism need not necessarily involve change of residence. Greenwood clearly brings this into focus when he defines tourism as basically a form of recreation expressed either through travel or through a temporary change of residence (Greenwood, 1976). Pearce expressed a similar viewpoint, when he defined tourism as, "The relationship and phenomena arising out of the journey and temporary stays of people travelling primarily for leisure or recreation."

Sometimes there is need to define tourism in a wider sense. Obviously, all forms of travel are not tourism. A daily commuter travelling between his suburban residence to the place or work in the city is not a tourist. But, if on any weekend the same person takes his children to the city museum or zoo, he will be regarded as a tourist. By the same logic, a student going abroad to pursue higher study is not a tourist. He is more likely to have a student visa and his period of stay usually continues upto the completion of his study. But, the same student may turn into a tourist when he spends his holiday by visiting the places of interest of his host country. Even a person attending a summer or winter school away from his usual place of residence would not be a tourist in the narrow sense, since the purpose of his temporary change of residence is not pure recreation. But, in many studies relating to international tourism, foreign students are regarded as tourists. Similarly a journalist going to cover the Olympic games or similar meets should not be termed as tourists although such visitors are on at par with other tourists from the consideration of foreign exchange earning by the host country. Now-a-days business officials travelling internationally are also called 'business tourists', although they are not tourists according to the above definitions.

A pertinent question that may be raised here is whether we should bring in the motivational aspects at all. Often persons of different motivations for travel behave in the same way. For instance, a business executive attending business convention or a scientist attending a seminar may also spend a part of his time in sightseeing, visiting nightclubs or making local shopping trips just like an ordinary tourist with pleasure as his main motivation.

Another feature of tourism, not adequately addressed is how long the duration of stay should be. As a usual practice, a stay of at least 24 hours is considered necessary to distinguish a tourist from a day-tripper. According to Pearce, there could be no hard and fast rule regarding duration of stay. Realizing the growing importance of collecting tourist statistics, the League of Nations defined in 1937 the term 'foreign tourist' as "any person visiting a country, other than that in which he usually resides for a period of at least 24 hours." According to this definition the following persons were to be considered tourists:

- Persons travelling for pleasure, for domestic reasons, for health etc.
- Persons attending meeting of any kind.
- Persons travelling for business purpose.
- Persons arriving in the course of a cruise, even when stay for less than 24 hours.

In 1963, a revised definition was prepared and adopted at the

UN Conference on International Travel and Tourism held in Rome. It considered an overall definition of the term 'visitor', which for statistical purpose describes, "any person visiting country other than that in which he has his usual place of residence, for any reason other than following an occupation remunerated from within the country visited."

This definition covered: Tourists, i.e. temporary visitors staying at least 24 hours in the country visited and purpose of whose journey can be classified under one of the following headings:

- Leisure (recreation, holiday, health, study, religion and sport).
- Business, family, mission, meeting.
- Excursionists, i.e. temporary visitors staying less than 24 hours in the country visited (including travellers on cruises).

The above definition excludes the transit passengers. These passengers are usually allowed to stay few days or hours and visit the country. Taking all these considerations into account, it is not difficult to see why the most popular and widely accepted definition of tourism is one defined by the World Tourism Organization (WTO). According to that definition: A tourist is a person who travels to a place other than his usual place of residence and stays at hotels and other accommodation establishments run on a commercial basis (or in rent free places) for a duration of not less than 24 hours and not more than six months at a time, for any of the following purposes:

- Pleasure
- Pilgrimage
- Study and health
- Meetings
- Business.

Economics of Leisure and Types of Tourism

Aristotle drew a distinction between work, play and leisure. He defined work as something, which one does for something else (livelihood). Play was mere reaction for work. He deemed leisure as higher and nobler than work and play, defined it as "the employment of time in an activity for its own sake." This concept of leisure has a great influence in determining the mood of mass tourism.

Veblen was the first economist who discussed the value of the leisure class as an economic factor in modern life. As early as in 1899 in his celebrated book *The Theory of the Leisure Class* he captured the phenomenon and gave a theoretical foundation for the first time. Tourism from those days of conspicuous consumption travelled a long path. The nature of consumption too changed a lot. Only hundred years back hunting in the forest or killing 50,000 birds a day at Bharatpur sanctuary (India) was a much-professed pleasure of the native kings and Viceroys in India. Bharatpur today is a celebrated bird sanctuary and *Ramsar site* wetland.

From motivational point of view, a distinction can be made between a recreational tourist and a motivated tourist. The primary urge of the first type of tourist is travel for pleasure with its entertainment value or recreation as an end in itself. The primary urge of a motivated tourist may be altogether different. To him travelling for pleasure is there but not as a primary motive.

Be it recreation or pleasure, a distinction can be made between two polar types. Some tourists make a careful selection of the spot where the entire holiday or any leisure time is spent. Holiday homes or cottages cater to such resort tourists. On the other end, there are tourists with wanderlust. Their tour itinerary covers as many spots as possible seeking different culture, cuisine or ways of life all packed in a short period of time. Travel companies and tour operators with their pre-paid package tours cater to the latter type of tourists. The adage, 'If it is Tuesday, it must be Belgium' is applicable to them.

Table 2.1
Characteristic Features of Various Types of Tourist

Sl. no	*Type of tourist*	*Destinations*	*Price elasticity*	*Sea-sonality*	*Length of stay*
1	*2*	*3*	*4*	*5*	*6*
1.	Resort tourist	Beach resort, hill station	High	Highly seasonal	Average (i.e. 10 to 15 days)
2.	Wanderers	Big cities, historical sites etc.	High	Highly seasonal	Average
3.	Delegates/ Participants	Places of event, conference etc.	Low	Seasonal	Normally below average
4.	Business	Big cities depending on job	Inelastic	Negligible	Generally below average
5.	Pilgrim	Holy places	Low	Fairly seasonal	Normally average
6.	Health	Health resort or big city	High	Normally seasonal	Normally average
7.	Family visitor	Any where	Inelastic	Seasonal	Longer stay

The tourism experience is like a durable consumer good. But, the perishability character of a tourism experience depends only on time and not on the rate of utilization. In case of a tourist product, the law of diminishing marginal utility may not apply in all cases. For example, the satisfaction derived in the high altitude Himalayan trails or sunbathing on sandy beaches is likely to increase as a consumer adjusts to the surrounding.

Price elasticity of tourism demand, seasonality of tourist traffic, duration of stay or frequency of visit vary widely for the different types of tourist. For instance, the resort tourists are more responsive to the price level than the wanderlust. Similarly, average length of stay of a business tourist is lower than that of a resort tourist although the expenditure per day of a business tourist is much higher than the latter.

EXERCISES

1. How far do you think R. De Meyer's definition of tourism lacks precision?
2. Why Bernecker's definition is considered too precise?
3. How WTO defines a tourist?
4. Which of the followings are considered as tourists? Give reasons.

   (*i*) A commuter coming daily from his residence at Kalyan to Noriman Point (Bombay) to attend his office.
   (*ii*) Mr. Banerjee spent two days and one night in a Calcutta hotel to enjoy Durgapuja Festival.
   (*iii*) Daud Ibrahim, a 'wanted' citizen with arrest warrant in India visits Dubai.
   (*iv*) Profesor Taro Yamane, travelling to Sarnath enroute to Kathmandu after attending a conference at Indian Institute of Technology, Kharagpur.
   (*v*) Mr. Tajuddin Ahmed, a citizen of Bangladesh getting treated at Apollo Hospital, Chennai.

5. 'Tourism experience is like a durable consumer good'—explain the statement.
6. What do you mean by price elasticity of tourism?
7. Discuss whether the following statements are true or false:

(*i*) Importance of seasonality for the wanderers is negligible.
(*ii*) Elasticity of the pilgrim tourists is low.
(*iii*) Destination for health tourists is normally seaside.
(*iv*) Most of the international tourists prefer developed world.
(*v*) Tourists by and large do not care for terrorism.

8. What do you mean by 'tourist night'? To what extent 'tourist night' is different from number of 'tourist visit'?
9. What is the difference between a transit tourist and a vacationer?

Chapter Three
Economic Rationality

Economic Rationale for Third World Tourism

From an economic point of view, tourism seems to play two major yet distinct roles in the overall economic development: (*a*) as a parameter of development of backward resource poor areas and (*b*) as a source of earning scarce foreign exchange.

To understand the economic rationale it is important to distinguish the difference between developed and underdeveloped countries. In the developed countries process of industrialization had been accompanied by the absorption of the surplus rural population into the expanding urban industrial centers. This also helped the process of structural reorganization of the rural production sector in the wake of industrialization. In the developing countries the urban industrial sector has not developed sufficiently even to fully absorb the growing urban labour force. A familiar feature of a labour surplus third world economy is that in the process of technological progress, a significant part of the labour force fails to get involved in gainful employment in the organized sector due to the lack of appropriate skills required in the changed situation.

But from society's point of view, the unemployed human resources are the fixed costs borne by the society that cannot be escaped. J.M. Clark was perhaps the first economist who looked at the problem of unutilized human resources in terms of overhead cost (Clark, 1943). The society does not altogether avoid the cost of maintenance of an unemployed labour when he is forced to live on a subsistence level and on a park bench. However, the society bears the cost of this deterioration.

With this reality tourism may come forward with considerable opportunity of capital formation in countries, which have sufficient advantage in either geography (Australia, Canada, U.S. and Brazil) or history (Greece, Israel) or even both (India and China). Many of the tourism success countries of Europe have built their fortune by selling their history to the visitors. India for example has plenty of tourist products starting from lofty beaches to the great Himalayas or even the ancient history. But commercial thrust of these rare tourism resources is by far conspicuously absent.

To most people, tourism does not appear as a 'basic need' or even as a merit or 'priority good'. To a great extent this is the legacy of the earlier association of tourism for recreation with the leisure class. But from the economist's point of view, the pertinent question is not whether tourism is socially useful or not, but whether the resources used for developing tourism has a more socially useful way of utilization with a comparative advantage counting in the benefit side of the balance. That is the beneficial effects of utilization of otherwise non-utilized human resources.

Tourism not only increases the possibility of absorbing more readily available skilled or semi-skilled working forces, it also makes much better and economic use of certain other resources with low opportunity costs. For example, some natural sites that offer scenic view, temperate climate or wildlife if left as it is they are not usually expected to be exploited except maintaining the bio-diversity and ecology. But tourist attraction here is a net contribution to the economy without destroying the very source.

Agent of Regional Development

The problem of regional development in the under-developed areas has been analyzed by a number of economists. There is hardly any disagreement on the point that in the early stage of economic development, concentration of development in a few centres would take place unavoidably. As the economy grows into a mature one, the spread effect of development from the core areas would reach wider areas. At this point economists are led to two opposite conclusions. While Freedman and Alonso (1965) agreed that spread effects would tend to reduce regional disparities, Hirschman (1958) and Myrdal (1972) on the other hand, observed that there was every chance that the backwash effects in under-developed economies could swamp the spread effect.

Resources like flora and fauna like Jaldapara (India), or Masaimara (Kenya); beach resorts like Pattaya (Thailand) or Cox bazaar (Bangladesh); ruins like, Mohenjodaro (Pakistan) or Great Wall (China) or the peak like Mount Everest of Nepal are price less. Nevertheless, these are either free gifts or part of cultural heritage considered as fixed asset. The temperate climate of the Himalayan villages or the cultural values of the Pyramid are not things to be imported. Furthermore, tourist centers in most of the developing countries are mostly located in untouched regions, usually in less favoured parts. Among them may be mentioned Khajuraho, Konarak, Ajanta-Ellora, Mandu, Humpi, Hallebid-Bellur in India; Mohenjodaro in Pakistan; Polonnaruwa and Singiriya in Srilanka; Angkor Vat in Kampuchea; or Borobudur in

Indonesia. With proper planning these far flung places may turn into Jet-set centers and attract foreign visitors in large scale. Khajuraho in India and Ixtapa-Zihuatanejo in Mexico are two such success stories.

Human Resource Development

Most of the developing countries suffer from population pressure and abundance of labour force not skilled in those lines for which there is a growing demand. Paucity of physical capital is also an important bottleneck to utilize such labour. As a result service sector gets inflated as a source of employment since labour absorption rate or labour- output ratio is relatively high in this sector than the primary or secondary sectors. As a service sector industry, tourism has certain advantages in absorbing locally available poor in the remote places of tourist importance. Labour intensive nature of tourism had been established in Hawaii (Leontief, 1956). Measuring the labour intensity as a ratio of man years of labour to $10,000 of capital, the three categories associated with travel: eating-drinking places, hotels and other personal services yield a labour capital ratio of 1.43 as compared to the ratio of 1.03 for services in general in Hawaii.

Besides, tourism is important in terms not only for the jobs it creates and sustains but also in the cost benefit ratio involved. This is because it employs resources with low or no opportunity costs. In small countries like Bermuda, Malta, Nepal, Srilanka, Maldives, Mauritius, Guam, Vanuatu and so on, shortage of physical resource and capital led them to the path of tourism development.

As tourism develops and hotels motels and resting places mushroom, local folks generally occupy the lowest rung of employment as waiter, busboy, room maid, gardener, kitchen helper and so on. In sophisticated jobs if the local people fail to acquire required skill they would be side tracked and outsiders would capture employment opportunities. The question of skill needs some explanation here. The high altitude porters who are available in great numbers in many Indian and Nepalese tourist spots do not possess any formal education. Nonetheless, they have a definite role in high altitude tourism in those regions. In some countries (Turkey or Egypt for example), just possession of a foreign language itself is a skill for which despite the existence of mass illiteracy they find employment in tourism-oriented activities. Thus, it is not the lack of innate ability or even the dearth of technical skill, but the lack of initiative or interest in improving their economic status that is to be counted as the most important stumbling block to progress (Myrdal, 1972).

Tourism as an Invisible Trade Item

The tourist product is by definition highly differentiated one, in which substitutability is possible but perfect substitution is not. As a result of this, the market is necessarily one of 'monopolistic competition', and the demand curve may in fact, vary abruptly, particularly due to natural and political upheavals. As observed by Tisdell (2005) despite the rapid growth of the modern tourism industry, it is an economically vulnerable industry. Business in significant segments of it finds that they have a high proportion of costs that are inescapable in the short run. In addition major and key portions of the industry operate in conditions akin to those under large group monopolistic competition. In long-term equilibrium they therefore have only normal profit, have excess capacity and operate at less than minimum efficient scale. This seems to be usual for hotels. However, even the airline industry appears to have been in a similar position prior to September 11, 2001.

Moreover, it is not entirely clear that, all tourist products are 'normal' goods in the sense that a reduction in price will *ceteris-paribus* raises demand. The most characteristic and seemingly paradoxical feature of tourism is that it represents trade in non-traded goods. It is therefore, a matter of surprise that tourism has so long been completely ignored by trade theorists.

Between 1995 and 2000, tourism receipts measured in US dollars have grown at six per cent per annum in Africa, 7 to 14 per cent in Central and South America, 6 per cent in Middle East and 7 per cent in South Asia. A summary of tourism receipts by region is given in Table 3.1.

Tables 3.2 and 3.3 show tourism receipts as a percentage of GDP in some selected countries. As can be seen from the tables, tourism is more important in middle-income and low-income countries. Of course within each group there are much variations, with some island economies deriving as much as 99 per cent of GDP directly from tourism.

Table 3.1
Tourism Receipts by Region and Average Growth

Receipts (US $ bn)

Country	*1990*	*1995*	*2000*	*1995-2000*
World	263.4	406.5	474.4	3.1
Africa	5.3	8.1	10.9	6.0
Americas	69.2	99.6	132.8	5.9
East Asia and Pacific	39.2	73.7	81.4	2.0
Europe	143.2	212.9	233.0	1.8
Middle East	4.4	8.7	11.5	5.8
South Asia	2.0	3.5	4.9	7.2

Source: World Tourism Organization.

Table 3.2
Tourism Receipts as Percentage of GDP

Country/region	*GDP US $ trillion (2001)*	*Tourism receipts US $ bn (2000)*	*Tourism receipts as share of GDP (%)*
High income	25.3	336.4	2.25
LDCs	6.2	139.3	1.33
Middle income countries	5.1	122.8	2.41

Selected developing countries

Country	*GDP US $ bn (2001)*	*Tourism receipts US$ mn (2000)*	*Tourism receipts as share of GDP (%)*
Azarbaijan	5.3	63.0	1.2
Cayman Islands	1.0	447.9	44.7
Colombia	83.2	1000.0	1.2
Congo DR	4.9	6.0	0.1
Ghana	5.0	386.0	7.7
India	457.0	3200.0	0.7
Oman	19.8	120.0	0.6
Seychelles	0.6	115.3	19.3

Source: Based on World Development Indicators.

Table 3.3
Tourism Receipts as Percentage of GNP and Exports in Some Selected Countries

Country	*Percentage of GNP*	*Percentage of exports*
Maldives	99.1	57.4
Antigua & Barmuda	83.3	83.3
St Lucia	45.9	63.4
Seychelles	31.0	43.2
Barbados	27.4	56.3
Jamaica	26.7	37.0
St. Vincent & Grenadines	24.9	41.5

(*Contd.*)

Country	Percentage of GNP	Percentage of exports
Belize	24.4	38.0
Malta	21.8	—
Grenada	18.1	38.0
Gambia	15.3	24.0
Fiji	14.8	24.3
Vanuatu	14.3	—
Dominican Republic	13.9	48.6

Source: IFC/World Bank (2000).

Table 3.4
International Tourism Arrivals and International Tourism Receipts by Regions in 2000 by Market Share in Percent

Region	Arrival (%)	Receipts (%)
Africa	4.0	2.2
Americas	18.5	28.7
East Asia/Pacific	16.0	17.3
Europe	57.7	48.6
Middle East	2.9	2.0
South Asia	0.9	1.1
Total	*100*	*100*

Source: WTO, 2000.

Table 3.5
Market Share in Terms of World International Tourist Arrivals for 2000 and as Predicted by WTO for 2020

Region	Market share in 2000	Market share in 2020
Africa	4.0	5.0
Americas	18.5	18.1
East Asia/Pacific	16.0	25.4
Europe	57.7	45.9
Middle East	2.9	4.4
South Asia	0.9	1.9
Total	*100*	*100*

Table 3.6
World's Top 15 Tourism Destinations Ranked by Number of International Tourist Arrivals

Rank	Country	International tourist arrivals (million)		Market share (%)
		1999	2000	2000
1.	France	73.0	75.5	10.8
2.	United States	48.5	50.9	7.3
3.	Spain	46.8	48.2	6.9
4.	Italy	36.5	41.2	5.9
5.	China	27.0	31.2	4.5
6.	United Kingdom	25.4	25.2	3.6
7.	Russian Federation	18.5	21.2	3.0
8.	Mexico	19.0	20.6	3.0
9.	Canada	19.5	20.4	2.9
10.	Germany	17.1	19.0	2.7
11.	Austria	17.5	18.0	2.6
12.	Poland	18.0	17.4	2.5
13.	Hungary	14.4	15.6	2.2
14.	Hong Kong (China)	11.3	13.1	1.9
15.	Greece	12.2	12.5	1.8
	INDIA	2.5	2.6	.4

Source: WTO, 2002, Reserve Bank of India.

EXERCISES

1. Explain the role of tourism as an agent of development in far-flung and remote areas of the developing countries.
2. 'International tourism is an important source of foreign exchange more in a small country than a large one'—explain the statement.
3. Discuss whether the following statements are true or false:

   (*i*) In a country like India to most people, tourism does

not appear as a 'basic need' or even as a merit or 'priority good'.

(*ii*) In countries of low domestic capital formation, higher the growth of international tourism lower is the import content of tourist earning.

(*iii*) Trade theorists have never ignored tourism.

(*iv*) International tourism is nothing but selling the country abroad as invisible tread item.

(*v*) South Asia is one of the poorest regions of the world but average growth of tourism receipts is highest here.

4. Suppose, Mr. Smith is a wanderer tourist and likes to travel in the Himalayas. He has two options: Nepal Himalayas and Indian Himalayas. Being a comfort and time conscious tourist what country he would choose? Justify your answer.
5. Why tourist market is necessarily one of 'Monopolistic Competition'?
6. Given the fact that average length of stay of a foreign tourist in Thailand is 5 days and that of a foreign tourist in India is 26 days find the tourist bed night figures when number of visitors in Thailand and India are 4 million and 2.5 million respectively. Comment on the result.

Chapter Four

Determinants of Tourism Demand

Demand for tourism consists of three major components: actual or effective demand, potential demand and deferred demand (Mathieson and Wall, 1982). Effective demand is synonymous with the actual number of visitors. Potential demand includes tourism minded people who are unable to travel due to financial constraints or some other reason. Finally deferred demand means those people who lack the knowledge of location, communication and so on. Both potential and deferred components are extremely difficult to measure. Hence, the concept of effective demand is frequently used for demand estimation.

Application of Operations Research

Operations Research (OR) is a term which stands for an approach to problem-solving characterized by a systems orientation, an interdisciplinary philosophy. This implies the quantitative modelling and manipulation of these models through the use of mathematical, statistical and computer methodologies in order to solve decisions, plans and policies.

Within the field of tourism, the term OR appears to be first used in the literature by Cesario (1969). The most researched areas of tourism for the application of OR are tourist forecasting, determination of tourist flows, the measurement and evaluation of the impact of tourism etc.

From an Operational Research viewpoint, forecasting models are often classified as being causal, time series or quantitative in nature. One of the primary motivators behind the consideration of developing tourism potential is the expectation that, once developed, an income stream will be generated that can then be used to enhance the region's other economic sectors. As such, the measurement of this income stream is the most traditional measure of tourism impact. In more recent work, the need to consider the social, cultural and political impact of tourism has been felt. However, the state of the art is such that there are only a few documented cases where the quantitative evaluation of these impacts has been successful. Mostly used approach of evaluating tourism is based on classical economic theories.

Among the deterministic approaches, Gearing, Swart and Var (1978) also developed a tourism flow model as part of a multiperiod planning model for tourism development. The basic hypothesis in their model is that the development of new projects changes the "touristic attractiveness" of a region and that, as a consequence, existing tourist flows will be redistributed to reflect this change. The concept of "carrying capacity" is explicitly incorporated into the model.

A specific example to illustrate the stochastic approach is given by Mednick (1975), who has designed a model designed to describe the probabilities that US visitors to the province Ontario would make overnight stops among the ten economic regions of the province. The model is a Markov chain whose transition probability matrix illustrates the relationships of the economic regions as locations of overnight stopping points.

Use of Linear Programming Method

Economic impact studies of tourism are growing in popularity for a variety of reasons. First, as tourism activities develop, environmental (both social and physical) side effects may occur (Foster, 1964; Greenwood, 1976; Cohen, 1978). In fact, economic development activities rely on the use of natural resources and usually have significant effect on environment. Consequently, municipalities and other local bodies find it important to conduct economic impact studies. Second, impact studies can restrict or counter the industries wishing influence legislation through lobbyists by documenting economic viability of an industry. For example, a strong lobby of industrialists or vested interests may argue in favour of an industry at a place ignoring the long run effect of the unit. The economic impact study may incorporate the opportunity cost or even environmental cost and counter the argument put forward by the above-mentioned industrialists. Third, it helps in identifying the sources and extent of revenue to the local administrations. Municipal and regional planning officials are often faced with problems in making decision on alternative tourism developments. While this may be good for the economy, the community in question may still wish to place some constraints on the use of its limited sources. These constraints on choice can be presented as a set of linear inequalities.

The Concept

Linear Programming (LP) as an approach is basically entrusted in maximizing a linear objective function given a set of linear inequalities. The best technique to solve such a problem would be LP Model formulated according to the objective. Choice faced by the planners can be formulated as an objective function and constraints on choice can be presented as a set of linear inequalities.

One advantage of LP is that a problem can be modelled to represent choices among types of firms or recreation centres. In any planning exercise relating to tourism, these may be important considerations. Another advantage is that a variety of constraints such as limited resources, maximum capacities etc., can be included to represent realistic situations.

One useful assumption of such LP approach is that an actual existing situation can provide an appropriate benchmark from which a proposed change in development might occur. An LP framework based on these assumptions can give economic planners at the local level an opportunity to monitor on-going development.

For some time now, LP has been used for solving problems involving private enterprise. But in the case of tourism, an obvious objective would be to maximize benefits including things like gross income, tax revenue or number of tourists. Kottke (1987) applied this technique in New London county situation in 1982. In one study on Digha, a seaside resort of West Bengal, India the LP approach was tested with the objective of maximizing the revenue from different sources of earning like accommodation, parks and so on (Chattopadhyay and Neogi, 2004).

In order to test the applicability of LP for studying economic impact of tourism, a model can be constructed in such a way that it is representative of community's tourism industry and at the same time allows opportunities for controlled development.

Given these requirements, the following model can be formulated with the objective:

To maximize

$$Y = \sum_{j=1}^{n} C_j X_j + \sum_{k=1}^{p} P_K V_K$$

Subject to

$$\sum_{j=1}^{n} a_{ij} X_j + \sum_{k=1}^{p} a_{ik} V_k \leq B_i \qquad (i = 1, \ldots\ldots\ldots, M)$$

$$X_j = R_j \qquad (j = 1, \ldots, n)$$

$$X_J \geq 0$$

$$V_K \geq 0$$

Where,

Y = total gross income attributable to tourism
C_j = gross tourism income per benchmark firm
X_j = number of bench mark firm by type (*j*)
P_k = gross tourism income per new firm
V_k = number of new tourism firms
a_{ij} = input coefficient per benchmark firm
a_{ik} = input coefficient per new firm
B_i = quantity of resources available for use by the tourism industry or projected levels of tourists visits
R_j = number of existing tourism firms by type (*j*)

Case Study of Digha

Digha is a popular beach resort of West Bengal. It has sufficient ingredients necessary to be a success in tourist industry. It offers a clean town, mile after mile hard flat beach. The gently rolling sea is almost screened from the town by thick Casuarinas forest. The character of Digha's tourism has been shaped by the nearness of the large metropolis Calcutta. With fixed physical supply of land including beach and forests, what is important for Digha is a careful planning for future development.

The benchmark situation was designed around Digha in 1988-89. It consisted of 230 tourism firms or enterprises. Of these firms, 126 accommodation units, 50 eating and drinking places, five local transport, four recreation units, 25 shopping and souvenir centres and 20 other support business units were identified.

As per local Master Plan, a total of 1575 acres of land was used for tourism development. Of these, 225 acres of beach area was estimated with assumption of the availability of half the breadth between high tide and low tide water. Over 1.5 million tourists were estimated for benchmark situation. Of these, about one million visits were at halting places and rests were day-trippers.

In applying the model to the benchmark situation, five activities, three constraints and one transfer equation were included. It is to be noted that the benchmark situation was not intended to be an optimal solution. Rather, it was to serve as a base for comparing projected solutions.

Most of the data required for applying the model to the benchmark situation are provided in Table 4.1. Here in addition to the constraints, aspects like soil condition, land use pattern, silting and marine erosion, sanitation etc., were also considered. Three projected growth situations were specified for the testing applicability of the model. In the first situation tourist growth was assumed to be 50 per cent with no restriction of accommodation unit. In the second situation accommodation unit was restricted to increase by 50 per cent only, tourist growth remaining the same. In the third situation tourist growth was assumed to grow by 25 per cent. Upper bound of accommodation units remained same (i.e. 50 %). Time period was uniform in all the three cases, which was 10 years. The LP solutions observed are shown in Table 4.3.

The merit of this LP study can be challenged from many grounds. The benchmark situation, with which the projected situations are compared, may be quite old. Upper bound fixation is subjective. The competing industries or activities in the same spots are not considered in optimizing the objective function. For example, in case of a beach resort the fishing industry and similar other industries like coconut cultivation are generally ignored. Nevertheless, the model shows successful empirical and operational procedure for evaluating alternative tourism development proposals at a practical quantitative level.

Table 4.1
Benchmark Situation for Digha Tourism

Name of activities/constraints Recreation centres or support business activity	*Number of firms*	*Average gross income per firm (000 Rs)*
Accommodation	126	200.00
Food and drink	50	320.00
Camping sites	6	10.00
Parks	6	12.00
Local transport	10	72.00
Coastal urban	1575	
Coastal rural	5006	
Total Employment	6581	
Full time	3800	
Seasonal	1200	
Total	5000	
Visit by tourists (number in thousand)	1400	
Gross income (Rs.)	42,052,000.00	

Table 4.2
Projected Growth Situation with Limitation and Time Period

Projected growth situation	*Projected growth in tourism visit (%)*	*Upper bound of accommodation units*	*Plan period (years)*
A	50	Nil	10
B	50	50	10
C	25	50	10

Table 4.3
LP Solution for Situations A, B, C as Proposed in the Study

Activities and constraints	*Quantity in number*			*Percentage change from benchmark*		
	Situations			*Situations*		
	A	*B*	*C*	*A*	*B*	*C*
Solutions:						
Accommodation	103	50	50	97	40	40
Food and drink	17	26	9	34	52	18
Constraints:						
Land use (acre)	650	650	650	50	50	50
Employment	1000	1000	1000	20	20	20
Number of tourist	700000	700000	350000	50	50	25
Gross income (Rs)	26040000	18300000	1288000	62	43.5	30

Application of Data Envelopment Analysis

Data Envelopment Analysis (DEA) is a multivariate technique for monitoring productivity and providing some insights into possible ways to improve the status quo, when inefficient. DEA is a non-parametric technique; that is, it can compare input/output data making no prior assumptions about the probability distribution under study. While LP method is used to maximize an objective function with given constraints and is typically determined by a specific equation, DEA is generated from the data set of observed operative units (Decision-Making Units or DMUs). The DEA efficiency score is derived from the comparison with the other DMUs that are included in the analysis, considering the maximum score of unity (or 100%) as a benchmark.

In 1986 DEA was first applied to the hospitality industry (Banker and Morey, 1986), specifically to the restaurants. Corporate travel management has been analyzed in Bell and Morey (1995). Morey and Dittman (1997) and Anderson *et al.* (2000) considered hotel sector in their studies of DEA. Bosetti, Cassinelli and Lanza conducted another interesting work on the relative performance of 70 municipalities' tourism management located on the coasts of Italy in 2002.

In the Italian study DMU represented a municipality producing the tourism good given two different inputs. The first was the cost of managing tourism infrastructures and, more generally, of the production of tourism services. The second was the environmental cost deriving from the increased number of people depending on the same environmental endowment. Thus on the input side, management and environmental costs had to be captured. On the output side, an indicator measuring the rate of use of existing beds had been used as a general approximation of profit deriving from the tourist industry. The number of beds was considered as an approximation for management expenses, while as an indicator of environment costs, data on yearly tons of solid waste produced in each municipality had been collected.

Multiple Regression Model

From the Operations Research viewpoint causal forecasting models are those, which explicitly attempt to quantify the relationship between a set of causal or independent variables and variable of interest (Swart, Var and Gearing, 1978). All regression and econometric models fall into this category. The Multiple Regression Model is fashioned after such causal forecasting model for international tourist flow developed by the Battle Research Centre in Geneva, Switzerland (Armstrong, 1972). The model hypotheses a simple relationship between the numbers of tourists annually generated to one country (*h*) by generating country's (*g*) number of population, and per capita GNP (PCI). Thus, the main objective here is to identify the factors, which influence most, the international tourism demand for h.

Conceptual Model

In neo-classical consumer demand theory, a tourist is a consumer who derives satisfaction (utility) from a vector of goods and services, which range from food and medical to travel and recreation. He distributes his known budget across the goods and services available at given prices for getting maximum utility. The individual demand for tourism originates from a budget allocation process, which maximizes utility. Thus, we can set-up the following utility maximization condition:

$$\text{Max } U(Q, R) \qquad \ldots(1)$$

Subject to the budget constraint

$$P_q Q + P_r R = Y \qquad \ldots(2)$$

Where U = utility function, Q = tourism related goods, P_q = price of Q, R = all other goods and services, P_r = price of R. Y. = total budget (income). Although time is a valuable factor in the sense its opportunity cost exists, it is ignored in the model. By solving Lagrange multiplier,

$$L = U(Q, R) - \lambda (P_q Q + Pr\, R) \qquad \ldots(3)$$

One can now derive the following tourism demand equation.

$$Q = Q(P_q, P_r, Y) \qquad \ldots(4)$$

According to the travel cost demand model (Kealy and Bishop, 1986), cost of tourism related trip (P_q) varies with distance. The per capita income of tourist supplying countries also provides a measure to determine the budget of the tourist. In addition linguistic affinity (L_{hg}) is also an important determinant for the selection of a destination. Hence, equation (4) can be rewritten and applied to an international tourism demand function of any host country:

$$Q_{hg} = Q(Y_g, D_{hg}, L_{hg}, P_g) \qquad \ldots(5)$$

Where,

Q_{hg} = number of visitors visiting host country *h*,
Y_g = PCI of country *g*,
D_{hg} = distance between *g* and *h*,
L_{hg} = Linguistic affinity
P_g = number of population of country *g*.

From the above conceptual model, one can hypothesize that:

$dQ_{gh} / dY_g > 0$
$dQ_{hg} / dD_{hg} < 0$
$dQ_{hg} / dL_{hg} > 0$
$dQ_{hg} / dP_q > 0$

Given the composition of tourist generating countries in India, it has been observed that visitors come from both distant and neighbouring countries but tourists from Latin American countries are small in number. Hence in Indian study this distance factor was excluded (Chattopadhyay, 1995). Like-wise language factor was also ignored in order to avoid dummy complexities. Thus, one is left with only population and PCI. Although the basic tourism demand model is utility theoretic, a wide range of tourism studies are also based on direct parameterization of theoretical variables (Diamond, 1977; Johnson and Suits, 1983). The study on India was based on the use of double log specification of the tourism demand equations. Thus, equation (5) can be written as—

$$LQ = \alpha_0 + \alpha_1 LY + \alpha_2 LP + \in \quad \text{.... (6)}$$

Where,

LQ = Log of Q
LY = Log of PCI
LP = Log of number of population
∈ = A stochastic error term

Empirical Results

The results of the analysis (OLS estimates) are reported in Table 4.4. Here PCI of selected countries are taken as independent variables. From the table regression estimates of PCI variables are found to be significant for 11 countries. However, for some countries the PCI coefficients were negative. That means tourist flows to *h* (here India) declined as per capita income of country *g* (here Canada, Srilanka and Poland) increased. Among them result of only Poland appeared significant. An increase in PCI can also be interpreted as an increase in the effective demand for visitors of country *g*.

Regarding number of population, eight countries were found to be significant in their coefficient values. For more than three fourth of the selected countries coefficient values were found positive. Negative values were observed for six countries indicating that greater the number of population in country *g*, smaller is the number of tourist from that country. Among these countries Spain, Italy and Hong Kong came up with significant values.

The result implies that countries with significant positive coefficients for per capita income are Austria, Germany, Spain, Italy, Switzerland, Sweden, UK, Singapore and the Gulf reflecting impressive response in selecting India as their destination. Being a country with less pronounced seasonality and offering tourist products of non-homogenous nature, India is relatively less exposed to the threats in terms of seasonality, variety or direction. Nevertheless the country's share of international visitors is palpably low than even many of her small neighbours. India has never been sold as holiday destinations. While only a meager percentage of the visitors come to enjoy beaches here (0.67 %), about 40 per cent come for site seeing (ISI, 1982). It has been observed from different studies (IIPO, 1978; Chib, 1981) that Germans spend 3.5 times as much as the French on foreign travel. In India they spend about 1.5 times as much as the French. France has its own resorts on the Mediterranean, but the beach loving Germans get few warm water beaches in their own country and go abroad for beach holiday. India also receives more French than Germans. The result also suggests that the elasticity estimates and population vary significantly from negative values to highly elastic measures. India's tourism market also appears to be extremely dominated by English knowing, commonwealth and high-income countries.

Table 4.4
Parameter Estimates of Selected Variables on the Number of Tourists Visiting India from Selected 25 Countries between 1971-1988

Sl. No	*Country*	*R^2*	*PCI (X1)*	*Population (X2)*	*Constant*
1.	Canada	0.9656	-2.8307 (3.5052)	16.550 (7.6086)	-23.354 (0.1391)
2.	USA	0.9394	1.1897 (3.5882)	3.4923 (6.0735)	-25.732 (3.9338)
3.	Austria	0.9659	2.2359 (0.6085)	65.896 (15.677)	-151.67 (27.714)
4.	Belgium	0.9014	0.3732 (1.9279)	61.881 (31.204)	143.00 (55.015)

(*Contd.*)

Sl. No	Country	R2	PCI (X1)	Population (X2)	Constant
5.	France	0.8467	8.8089 (5.8631)	-23.850 (26.838)	17.575 (53.939)
6.	FRG	0.9246	3.7048 (0.5774)	12.077 (11.246)	-80.186 (45.215)
7.	Italy	0.9551	13.287 (3.6160)	-88.276 (40.080)	236.71 (129.00)
8.	Spain	0.9072	11.452 (2.6814)	-18.626 (10.592)	-36.299 (19.779)
9.	Sweden	0.9618	4.1169 (0.4849)	-5.6486 (9.1096)	-24.434 (17.032)
10.	Switzerland	0.9680	3.2031 (1.2915)	15.233 (12.010)	55.416 (11.704)
11.	UK	0.9987	6.6178 (0.2280)	-32.601 (3.1039)	74.908 (10.566)
12.	Poland	0.9945	-7.9422 (2.2054)	36.772 (4.3656)	-73.042 (2.9247)
13.	Israel	0.5960	1.4070 (4.9202)	0.9229 (4.7674)	-13.728 (39.195)
14.	Jordan	0.9229	0.8406 (0.8132)	2.8599 (1.3914)	-8.8079 (4.4247)
15.	The Gulf	0.7956	4.5001 (1.6143)	2.2680 (0.7695)	-43.407 (15.106)
16.	Yemen	0.9799	3.0910 (0.5144)	1.0526 (1.1216)	19.592 (1.6968)
17.	Iran	0.9766	0.8252 (0.8709)	2.6234 (0.2636)	-13.272 (5.8976)
18.	Srilanka	0.9079	-0.9015 (1.3995)	5.9443 (2.2523)	-7.0153 (2.7504)
19.	Malaysia	0.8371	0.1376 (0.4908)	0.8170 (0.6453)	-0.7927 (2.0609)
20.	Singapore	0.9665	5.2175 (1.8771)	-2.2661 (3.0634)	-43.402 (14.659)
21.	Thailand	0.5954	0.7808 (3.3834)	1.1997 (5.7837)	-7.7604 (4.0394)
22.	Hong Kong	0.8604	15.3960 (4.4395)	-11.319 (4.6289)	-123.04 (33.834)
23.	Japan	0.9211	0.1484 (1.2260)	9.1276 (4.7729)	-41.507 (12.431)
24.	Australia	0.8268	0.5855 (4.3145)	3.3021 (5.4026	-11.266 (25.812)
25.	New Zealand	0.7523	3.0825 (6.7021)	0.3023 (18.291)	-27.462 (41.330)

— Figures in the parenthesis indicate standard error.

— Degree of freedom is 4.

Measuring Travel Propensity

The idea of unique selling proposition of a product or a range of products (and services) is as relevant to tourism as it is to the marketing of any consumer good. Market research on tourism is important to both travel agents as well as policy makers. The word market has several meanings depending, who use it? To the economist, it usually means all those buyers and sellers of goods and services who affect price. The market for tourism products in a country (a tourist generating area) can be stated as say one million people, or ten million journeys or one billion rupees or any combination of these.

Success in modern marketing calls for research into product development and consumers' requirements, tastes and preferences (Medlik, 1985). As Kottlar stated, 'Marketing's short-term task may be to adjust customer's wants to existing goods, but its long-term task is to adjust the goods to customer's wants (Kottlar, 1967). The popular Consumer Travel Decision (CTD) study deals with this short run task.

CTD study today is a very popular exercise for market research of tourism in countries where as an industry tourism is well-established. Sharp and Mott (1956) did one of the early studies on vacation behaviour. In their large investigation on consumer's purchase decision about car, housing, insurance, food budget and vacation areas at Detroit, the authors found that husbands and wives made 70 per cent of the vacation decisions jointly. Darden and Parreault (1975) tested the relationship between media exposure and consumer's life style and found these were more influential in determining vacation behaviour. A similar conclusion was drawn in an enquiry in income and level of living for selected occupational groups of city Calcutta (Chattopadhyay, Mukherjee and Rudra, 1989). In some studies vacation pattern of different communities were compared (Richardson and Crompton, 1988).

Covering the Ontario and Quebec residents, the authors carried out a study on vacation pattern with a view to identifying whether or not French Canadians and English Canadians differed in their vacation pattern. The CTD approach was attempted in the local study of Lincoln, Nebraska (Walter and Tong, 1977). In another study in Calcutta (Chattopadhyay, 1998), apart from decision pattern, an answer was being sought on the question of using statistical tools to predict travel behaviour. The study also established a relationship of respondents' income, family expenditure family size with CTD. Statistically significant relationships were found relating to monthly travel expenditure with monthly expenditure, age and income. Through multiple regression analysis, the prediction equation was found as:

$$Y = -0.0925 + 1.0135\,X1 + 1.9630 \times 2$$

Where,

Y = Average monthly expenditure on recreation travel,
X1 = Age,
X2 = Monthly income.

The correlation coefficient, *r* being 0.4.

In Calcutta study, 20 places of interest had been identified and the citizens were asked to mention the places they had visited. The study corroborated the observations of another earlier study done by Weightman (1987). She examined 13 group package tours to India and found that most of the foreign visitors were directed towards the north, the cities and the past. The domestic tourists too preferred Mughal influenced urban India.

Nature of vacation travel is an important determinant for successful marketing of a place. It was observed that while English Canadians appeared to travel significantly further and longer on their vacation trips than did French Canadians, French Canadians spent more per day than their English Canadian counterparts. This finding is consistent with the Canadian consumer behaviour literature (Mallen, 1977) that suggests that French Canadians consider travel an appropriate product for premium involvement. Similarly as mentioned earlier, it has been found that the Germans spend 3.5 times as much as the French on foreign travel but India gets more French than German tourists (Chib, 1981).

Appendix

With DEA methodology each DMU can freely assess its own set of weights, which can be inferred through the process of maximizing the efficiency. Given a set of N DMUs, each producing *J* outputs from a set of I inputs, let us denote by y_{jn} and x_{in} the vectors representing the quantities of outputs and inputs relative to the m_{th} DMU, respectively. The efficiency of the m_{th} DMU can thus be calculated as:

$$e_m = \frac{\sum_{j=1}^{j} u_j y_{jm}}{\sum_{i=1}^{I} v_i x_{im}}, \begin{bmatrix} j = 1, /...J/ \\ i = 1, /...I/ \end{bmatrix}$$

Where u_j and v_i are two vectors of weights that DMU *m* uses in order to measure the relative importance of the consumed and the produced factors. The set of weights in DEA is not given, but is calculated through the DMU's maximization problem stated below for the m_{th} DMU:

$$\text{Max } e_m$$

s.t

$$\frac{\sum_{j=1}^{J} u_j \quad y_{jn}}{\sum_{i=1}^{I} v_i \quad x_{in}} \leq \quad \forall n = 1, ...m, ...\text{N}$$

$$0 \le u_j \le 1$$
$$0 \le v_i \le 1$$

To simplify computation it is possible to scale the input prices so that the cost of the DMU *ms* inputs equals 1, thus transforming the problem set in (the above equation) into the ordinary linear programming problem stated below:

$$\text{Max } h_m = \sum_{j=1}^{J} u_j v_{jm}$$

s.t

$$\sum_{i=1}^{I} v_i x_{im} = 1$$

$$\sum_{j=1}^{J} u_j y_{jn} - \sum_{i=1}^{I} v_i \quad x_{in} \le 0 \qquad \forall n = 1, \ldots m, \ldots \text{N}$$

$$\varepsilon \le u_j \le 1, \quad \varepsilon \ \le v_i \le \ 1, \varepsilon \ \in \Re^{+}$$

EXERCISES

1. Show how impact studies can restrict or counter the industries wishing influence legislation through lobbyists by documenting economic viability of an industry.
2. State the reasons of increasing popularity of Linear programming in planning exercises relating to tourism.
3. "The idea of unique selling proposition of a product or a range of products (and services) is as relevant to tourism as it is to the marketing of any consumer good."—justify the statement.

4. What do you mean by Consumer Travel Decision Pattern? Mention some studies done in measuring such patterns.
5. What is the difference between effective demand and potential demand for tourism?
6. If you were asked to project future demand of a tourist resort, what parameters you would choose. What is the justification of including environmental parameters in such exercise?

Chapter Five

Appraising Tourism Impact

Multiplier Studies

As has been stated earlier, researches in the economic aspects of tourism can be classified under two broad groups: impact studies and policy oriented studies. The more specific aim of impact studies is to quantify income or employment generation by tourist flow that has occurred at a tourist region in the immediate past. Here a very popular exercise is to calculate different type of multipliers—a widely used concept in economics.

One conventional economic argument of tourism is its role as an invisible trade item. Any tourist expenditure is an invisible export in that it creates a flow of foreign currency into an economy. This is also true in any regional economy of a domestic setting. A tourism multiplier is a measurement of this relationship between inflow of money and the amount of economic activity, which this expenditure creates within the area. The whole process is a continuous one with limited sequence. More specifically a tourism multiplier is a measurement of the additional activity created by an additional unit of tourist expenditure or, in the case of a reduction in expenditure, the incremental fall in economic activity created by an incremental fall in tourist expenditure.

The Concept

Although the early theory of multiplier is frequently attributed to the work of R.F. Kahn (1931) and Lord Keynes (1933), it is apparent from the literature that the development of multiplier theory owes much to a variety of economists' working in several countries over a period of at least thirty years prior to Kahn and Keynes. The earliest reference to the concept occurs in the work of Bagehot (1882). Other studies have been documented by several writers, notably Shackle (1951 and 1967), Wright (1956), Boserup (1969), Zinder (1969) and Archer (1977).*

Multiplier is a result of certain flow, or injection of some expenditure in a region. This expenditure (say X) has three components. When it is re-spent, component A re-spends extra turnover as payment for purchasing raw materials and other inputs. Some amount of money is spent as wage, rent or interest. This is represented as B. Finally; C gives the amount of leakage, which means payment to the area outside the region under study. This process of income generation is illustrated below:

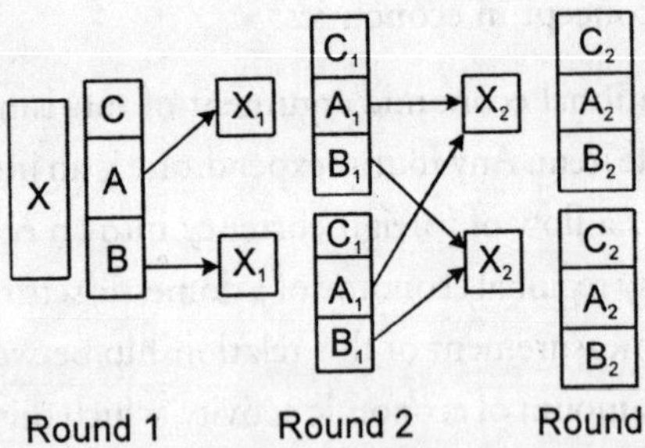

Of the principal flow of money three stay within the economy: the first forms public sector revenue; the second creates further domestic business activity and the third forms income to the

---

* For detail history of multipliers see Archer and Fletcher: Multiplier Analysis of Tourism, Centre Des Hautes Etudes Touristiques, April 1990.

resident population. In addition, the fourth flow, however, represents a loss of foreign currency to purchase imported goods and services. Such imports create a leakage of money out of the economic system and the magnitude of this leakage is an important factor in determining the size of the multiplier and the overall impact which tourism makes upon an economy. Smaller the import content of tourist services, higher will be the beneficiary effect of tourism in an economy.

One important segment of these three principal flows of money, which remain within the economic system, is domestic business sector. This sector too generates secondary economic activity. The revenue received by domestic retailers, wholesalers, manufacturers and importers in return for the goods and services which they have supplied to the hotels and other companies directly related to tourism is respent again with usual leakage.

It is difficult to generalize about how many rounds of transactions occur before leakages reduce the remaining money flows to a negligible amount because the situation varies widely from country to country and time to time. In USA as many as 13 or 14 rounds of transactions are measurable, whereas in small economies five or six rounds are sometimes sufficient to account for all of the measurable flows.

In round after round, this initial or primary injection of money produces two types of secondary effects: Indirect effect in terms of local purchase (A) and induced effect creating purchasing power to the owners of factors (B). These secondary effects are the essence of regional multiplier.

While there are different multiplier concepts, the following types are in common use:

- *Income multiplier*: It is a measure of total income generated by an extra unit of tourist expenditure. The multiplier coefficient when applied to the rupee equivalent of initial foreign exchange receipt yields an estimate of total rupee income, including income generated by induced expenditure.

- *Employment multiplier* : It can be expressed in one of two ways—as the ratio of combined direct and secondary employment generated by an additional unit of tourist expenditure to direct employment resulting from it or as total employment created by per unit incremental tourist expenditure.

Of these two types, what has been emerged to date, is that the effect of tourist spending is usually greater on employment than on income generation. Archer (1973) observed in Anglesey that an extra £10,000 of general spending generated 2.39 jobs compared to 4.83 jobs for £ 10,000 of tourist spending, whereas income effect of the two types of expenditure was approximately the same. This labour intensive nature of travel related expenditure was also established in another study done by Leontief (1956). Measuring the labour intensity as a ratio of man-years of labour to $ 10,000 of capital, the three categories associated with travel (eating and drinking places, hotels and other personal services) yielded a labour capital ratio of 1.43 as against ratio of 1.034 for services in general. The study was done in Hawaii.

Another study of tourism in Carlisle and Kendal by Archer (1979) is worth mentioning. The two case studies provided further evidence of the considerable importance of tourism to the economy of Cumbria. In 1978 over 219,000 visitors stayed in the two towns for a total of almost 4.5 million days. In addition over 420,000 day-trippers visited the towns.

The expenditure of these visitors in 1978 amounted to over 7.6 million pounds. This generated over 2.6 million pound of income to households in the two towns and a further 0.4 million pound to households living elsewhere in Cumbria. It also maintained over 1440 jobs in the two towns, of which about 58 per cent were permanent full time posts.

Models

There are four principal techniques available to measure the value of the multiplier: Base Theory Models, Keynesian Models, Ad hoc Models and Input-Output Analysis. The basic assumption underlying base theory models is that there is a stable relationship between each of the export sectors and the local sectors of an economy, so that changes in the level of tourist expenditure create predictable and measurable changes in the level of activity in local sectors. Base theory multipliers are normally over-simplified formulations and are very rarely used nowadays in practical research.

Most multipliers in common use incorporate the general principles of the Keynesian model. Keynes' basic model was:

$$K = \frac{1}{1-c+m} \qquad .....(1)$$

Where K is multiplier *c*, marginal propensity to consume and *m* marginal propensity to import. Here 1 is the additional unit of tourist expenditure and leakage is the proportion of this expenditure, which goes into savings (1–*c*) and import (*m*).

A long run formulation of this model may take into account the effects of investment and public sector spending. The effects are shown in equation (2)

$$K = \frac{1}{1-c+m-i-g} \qquad .....(2)$$

Here i is the marginal propensity to invest and g, marginal propensity of government expenditure. Archer (1976) derived a typical short run Keynesian multiplier as follows:

$$K = \frac{1-L}{1-c\,(1-t_i)\;(1-t_d-d)\;+m} \qquad \text{.....(3)}$$

Here, L is the first round leakage out of the country, t_i is the marginal rate of indirect taxation, t_d marginal rate of direct taxation and d being that of transfer payment.

If we assume some hypothetical values say L = 0.5, c = 0.9, m = 0.7, t_i = 0.1, t_d = 0.2 and d = 0.2, we get different values of multiplier for equations (1) and (3). For equation (1), it is 1.25 and for equation (3), it is 0.4118. Therefore, policy implications of the two multiplier-values would be different.

This revised model too has its limitations caused by leakages of each round of transactions. Hence, for practical solution a commonly used model has been developed known as Ad-hoc model. In principle it is similar to Keynesian approach. The simple form of the model is shown below:

$$K = A\,\frac{1}{1-BC} \qquad \text{......(4)}$$

Here A is percentage of tourist's spending retained in the region after first round leakage. B is propensity to consume of local people and C is the proportion of expenditure by local people that comes as income in the local economy. This approach has been widely used to trace the impact of tourism expenditure. The Ad-hoc model has been developed (Archer and Owen, 1971) as follows:

$$K = \sum_{j=1}^{N}\sum_{i=1}^{n} Q_j K_{ij} V_i \,\frac{1}{1-C\sum_{i=1}^{n} X_i Z_i V_i} \qquad \text{.....(5)}$$

Where,

Qj = Proportion of total tourist expenditure of jth category.

K_{ij} = Proportion of total tourist expenditure of jth category in ith type of business establishment.

V_i = Direct and indirect income generated by ith type of business establishment.

X_i = Proportion of total consumer expenditure by the residents of the locality by the ith type of business establishment.

Z_i = Proportion of total economic expenditure that takes place within the locality of the study.

C = Marginal propensity to consume.

Unlike the Keynesian and Ad-hoc multiplier models, input-output models present a general rather than partial approach. It provides a table of three components: an inter industry matrix showing sales and purchases of different sectors or industry's (sector's) purchase of primary inputs and finally purchases made by each sources of final demand. To explain this structure more clearly a simplified input-output framework of a four sector-economy may be considered. Suppose industry 1 is shown as buying or using a_{11} from its own production, a_{21} from industry 2; a_{31} from industry 3 and a_{41} from industry 4. In addition industry 1 buys p_1 from factors of production and m_1 from imports. Thus, the total purchases of industry 1 in the time period shown on the table are $a_{11} + a_{21} + a_{31} + a_{41} + p_1 + m_1 = X_1$

$$i.e. \sum a_{il} + p_l + m_l + X_l$$

At the same time industry 1 sells or uses a_{11} of its own product and sells a_{12} to industry 2, a_{13} to industry 3, a_{14} to industry 4, c_1 to consumer and y_1 to exports. Thus its total sales are:

$$\sum_{j=1}^{4} a_{1j} + c_1 + y_1 = X_1$$

Other sectors (2 to 4) are treated on the same manner.

The essence of this simple model is that the basic economy is shown within the A matrix (a_{11} to a_{44}) and all other sectors are treated as exogenous (i.e. outside) the basic economy. By the use of simple matrix algebra, it is possible to trace the flow of additional tourist expenditure through the economy and to measure the impact, which it has upon each sector, as well as the amount of income, public sector revenue and imports created at each round of transactions.

The simplest formulation is shown in equations (6) and (7) where for ease of explanation all final demand (c and y) has been assumed to be a column vector (Y).

$$X = AX + Y \quad .....(6)$$

$$X - AX = Y$$

$$(I - A)\,X = Y$$

$$X = (I - A)^{-1}\,Y \quad .....(7)$$

To illustrate the process let us take a coefficient matrix of two by two I-O table.

Table 5.1
Input Coefficients

	Industry 1	*Industry 2*	*Local household expenditure*
1. Industry 1	0.05	0.15	0.14
2. Industry 2	0.2	0.3	0.26
3. Local household earnings	0.1	0.25	0.05
4. Import	0.65	0.3	0.55
5. Total inputs	1.00	1.00	1.00

Four cells enclosed by a broken line represent the inter-regional sales between industries. Now by simple matrix algebra, it is possible to consider extra tourist expenditure and estimate the impact, which it has upon each sector. From Table 5.1 we have the values of inverse matrix in equation (8).

$$\begin{bmatrix} 1.102 & .236 \\ .315 & 1.496 \end{bmatrix} \quad \text{.....(8)}$$

Now if we assume an additional tourist expenditure of Rs. 100 in industry 1, then it will create 100 × 1.102 = Rs. 110.2 of activity in industry 1 and activity worth of Rs. 100 × .315 = Rs. 31.5 in industry 2.

This I-O sequence can also be extended for estimating indirect and induced effects.*

Record of empirical researches on the impact of tourism is very poor in ASEAN countries in spite of the impressive growth of tourism there. Considering the countries Malaysia, Singapore and Thailand one study was conducted in 1983 (Sakai, Sakamoto and Toida, 1983). In the standard input-output model, the authors measured effects on gross output, employment and imports of an exogenous change in final demand such as an increase in tourists' spending.

Limitations of Multiplier Models

Each of these modelling techniques has several inherent problems arising from data deficiency and restrictive assumptions very often come as hindrances.

* The example is coined from the study of Archer.

Excepting the developed countries of Europe, North America or Australia, in many newly emerging and developing countries available published and unpublished data are rarely adequate to feed the more demanding models. Tourist expenditure is spread across several sectors in an economy and accurate surveys of visitors are needed to obtain an acceptable breakdown of this expenditure into its component parts. Many tourist regions lack the infrastructure of collecting these data. For an input-output model a strong database is of great value.

In popular macro-economic models multipliers can be static or dynamic in form. Static models assume linear consumption and production functions, absence of supply constraints and constant relative prices. Dynamic models have been constructed to remove some of these constraints. Both static and dynamic models are suitable only for short and medium term analysis. The sequences of tourist expenditure in many cases are pretty long.

Elasticity in all sectors and the absence of supply constraints assumes that the economy concerned has the unused capacity and unused resources to meet the demands generated by additional tourism expenditure. In some sectors capacity may already be fully utilized and there may not be sufficient labour available. In such cases, especially in the short run, further tourism expenditure creates inflation and some of the additional goods and services required may have to be imported. This happens in many small island destinations.

Size of Multiplier

Like capital output ratio, the size of multiplier varies from region to region. This is because the size depends upon the nature of an area's economy and especially upon the extent to which the various sectors of the economy are inter-linked in their trading patterns.

Economic theory suggests that the principal factors governing the magnitude of the income multiplier under different circumstances as follows:

- The pattern of tourist expenditure.
- The size of the economy.
- The linkages between the tourism establishments and other sectors of the economy.
- The value added in each round of transactions, especially the first round.
- The leakage, which occur into imports and savings and supply constraints within the economy.

A large number of tourism multiplier studies have been carried out during the 1970's and 1980's. Some earlier work in the field, for example Zinder (1969) and Strang (1970) suggested that the value for tourist multiplier was high relative to many other industrial sectors. But, for the lack of conceptual understanding some misleading results emerged. In some countries these results were taken seriously, which not only called for excess investment expenditure but also caused considerable damage to tourism research. Zinder in his study on the impact of tourism in eastern Caribbean failed to understand the difference between income and economic turnover. He also allowed insufficient leakage and only considered the value of transactions. As a result, some astonishing facts of 89 per cent and 47 per cent share of tourism in the national income of Antigua and Barbados respectively emerged. Brownrigg and Greig (1975) developed a dis-aggregated neo-Keynesian regional multiplier technique to provide differential income and employment multipliers. They are of opinion that despite the relatively low value of the tourist multiplier, it is nevertheless possible that some aspects of tourist development have a considerably greater impact than the average value suggests. In their empirical case study in the remote rural area of the Isle of Skye in the Highland of Scotland, they distinguished between the source and the process of income/employment generation (i.e. the multiplicand and multiplier). The income generated in the process (ΔY_T) is given by the following expression:

$$\Delta Y_T = k_r \sum_{c=1}^{N} L_c$$

Where $L_1 \ldots L_N$ refers to the local value added by tourist expenditure in the various sectors (*c*) of the local economy and K_r is the regional multiplier. The Skye study illustrates how the popular multiplier can be adapted and disaggregated to yield estimates of the differential effects of tourism on both local income and employment. This allows sectoral multipliers to be estimated without constructing a full I-O Matrix. Brownrigg-Greig technique can at least provide partial guidance in regional policy decisions.

However, overall Skye study suggests that the value of the tourist multiplier is relatively low. That is, if tourism is developed in a region to diversify an area's industrial structure, it does not anticipate a strong linkage so that other sectors will develop. Black and Mc Dowall (1967) in their study on local I-O table also arrived at the same conclusion.

Economic theory suggests various factors that govern the magnitude of income multipliers. Some of these factors are pattern of tourist expenditure, size of economy, nature of tourists, intersectoral linkages of tourism establishments, import and other linkages etc. Larger economies generally posses a wider range of economic activities and thereby provide greater amount of goods and services necessary for tourism industry. On the other hand, smaller countries have to rely to a large extent on imports.

It has been observed that measurable rounds of transaction varies from region to region, where it is the case for a country as a whole, the number of round is larger whereas for smaller countries or regions, transactions reduce the remaining money flows to a negligible amount quickly. While in U.S, as many as 13 or 14 rounds of transactions are available, in small economies, usually five or six rounds are observed.

Empirical studies on multiplier analysis are rare in India. There are innumerable spots where similar studies can be undertaken for studying economic impacts. Places like Ajanta-Ellora, Khajuraho, remotely located historical forts are such places which lack other industrial or commercial endowments required to become a growth centre. Tourism is a strong force here. From the Ford Foundation study on Kulu Valley (Sing, 1989) of the western Himalayas, it was found that the non-resident entrepreneurs of Punjab siphon off a sizeable amount of tourism based economic turnover there. But, there was no quantitative follow up multiplier study of secondary impact there.

Long ago, National Council of Applied Economic Research calculated one multiplier figure, a big figure indeed 3.7 (NCAER, 1975). They assumed average national savings rate as 20 per cent with MPS being in the neighbourhood of 28-30 per cent with no leakage. Next, incorporating 12 per cent import content or leakage the estimated value of the multiplier boiled down to 1/. 28+. 12 = 2.5 per cent.

In 1978-79 Indian Institute of Public Opinion (IIPO, 1978) did another important study. They arrived at the tourist multiplier on the basis of a detailed input-output matrix of the national economy. IIPO prepared a matrix of 60 sectors for 1978-79 on the basis of Planning Commission's Input-Output tables for the year 1968-69 and 1973-74. Using relevant coefficients of the constructed matrix the contributions of tourism to national income as measured by gross value added was estimated to have been Rs. 9010 million.

Surrogate Approaches

One approach towards measuring the benefit associated with the development of tourist accommodations and attractions is the development of a utility measure, which reflects the touristic attractiveness of a given area. Gearing, Swart and Var (1976) developed an approach for the quantification of the notion of touristic attractiveness by constructing a multi-attribute utility function. The approach required that the following be determined;

1. The criteria by which touristic attractiveness is judged.
2. The relative importance of those criteria one to another, as indicated by a series of numerical weights.

   Then, with these two requirements satisfied, it is possible to
3. employ the judgements of experts in making evaluations against these criteria and using these inputs to
4. compute a numerical measure of the "relative attractiveness" of the touristic area. This then is the utility value associated with the site.

The results of the procedure were used to support the planning activities of the Turkish Ministry of Tourism. In particular, a ranking was obtained for the 65 geographical areas in Turkey, which have been defined as touristic areas.

Another popular method for the assessment of impacts stemming from tourism projects is the application of Delphi technique. Delphi modelling is one of the more recent methods of long-term forecasting. The Rand Corporation pioneered the technique in the 1960s. This modelling is a means of reaching consensus among experts in the area of interest through administering a series of questionnaires, collating judgements, and providing feedback from each series of questionnaires to all participants. This is one of group judgemental methods, which have gained recognition for their value in forecasting and accepted widely for its potential contribution to Environmental Impact Assessment (EIA). Linstone and Turoff (1975) have defined Delphi as "a method of structuring a group communication process so that the process is effective in allowing a group of individuals as a whole to deal with a complex problem." Delphi technique has two major advantages. First, the expert opinion expressed stem from the individual, not from a group of individual in constant contact of each other where peer pressure and the desire to conform may alter greatly any prediction given. Second, because the Delphi technique guarantees anonymity, the method can aim at gaining a more candid response.

In 1976, the Canadian Government Office of tourism employed this Delphi technique. In round 1 of the Delphi survey, scenarios were introduced. These were intended to elicit qualitative and quantitative feedback from Round 1 panelists who were distributed into four separate panels: general, demand, resource and impact.

In the second round the members of the general panel were distributed among the demand, resource and impact panelists. For the results of this round, the respondents were asked to rate the probability of a scenario becoming reality by 1986. They were then invited to modify their scenarios to give them higher probabilities, or to provide other scenarios if they did not agree with any of those stated. In all cases, the scenarios in these questions were constructed from the composite responses of panelists in Round 1.

In the light of potential advantages of low cost, rapid response, and ease of administration, which Delphi offers, this technique was adopted in public policy towards urban regeneration and local tourism development in Bradford, UK (Green, Hunter and Moore, 1990). The Bradford City Council and its Economic Development Unit took up a century old Salts Mill. Illingworth Morris ceased all operations in 1986, after 130 years of textile manufacturing on the site. Salts Estates Limited, a private concern, which proposed to redevelop and reorientate the mill towards the visitor market, purchased the mill in 1987. The building with its 7,23,000 sq. ft. floor space itself is of major architectural importance.#

In India this technique was applied in eco-tourism studies of Calcutta Wetlands (Chattopadhyay and Mazumder, 2002) and in Arunachal Pradesh (Mitra and Chattopadhyay, 2003).

Other Econometric Modelling

Use of econometric modelling for estimating the contribution of visitor industry to economic growth has been one of the popular methods of tourism study. In his empirical study Ghali (1976) started with the basic growth model as follows:

$$Y = \alpha_0 + \alpha_1 (X/Y)_{t-1} + \alpha_2 i(I/Y)_{t-1} + \alpha_3 g (G/Y)_{t-1}$$

Where

x = rate of growth of export.
i = rate of growth of private investment.
g = rate of growth of government expenditure.

Isolating tourism, total export was disaggregated into two components—tourist expenditure (x_1) and other exports (x_2).

For detail discussion on Delphi see Green, Hunter and Moore (1990).

Thus we get:

$$x = x_1 (x_1/x)_{t-1} + x_2 (x_2/x)_{t-1}$$

Similarly, disaggregating investments in construction of hotels (I_1) and other construction (I_2), the rate of growth of total investment is:

$$I = i_1 (I_1/I)_{t-1} + i_2 (I_2/I)_{t-1}$$

Unlike export, the two components of investments were treated endogenous to the model and assuming first component, investment in hotel construction is directly dependent on tourism; it was assumed that planned investment in hotels I^p_1 is a linear function of the expected change in the number of visitors $(\Delta T)^*_t$

$$I^p_{1t} = \beta_0 + \beta_1 (\Delta T)^*_t$$

and the expected change in the number of tourists is an unbiased forecast of the actual change

$$i.e.\ (\Delta T)^*_t = (\Delta T)_t + \epsilon_t \qquad E(\epsilon_t) = 0$$

Further, it was assumed that there is a one-year lag between planning and realization of investment in hotels, which can be written as:

$$I_{1t} = \beta_0 + \beta_1 (\Delta T)_{t-1} + u_t$$

The second component of investment is only indirectly influenced by tourism. Here also lag between planning and realization is one year. This component of investment can therefore be expressed as:

$$I_{2t} = \gamma_0 + \gamma_1 Y_{t-1} + e_t$$

The only remaining variable endogenous to the model is the rate of change in state and local government expenditure. Here expenditure is a linear function of the lagged level of personal income.

$$G_t = \delta_0 + \delta_1 Y_{t-1} + v_t$$

Ghali concluded that given the growth experience of Hawaii during 1953-70 where personal income grew at an average annual growth rate of 8 per cent, by 1970, the level of personal income would have increased to $ 2852 million compared to $ 3441 million achieved with the growth of tourism.

EXERCISES

1. What is tourism multiplier? Explain with suitable equation the methods of finding tourism multiplier following Keynesian theory.
2. By the use of simple matrix algebra, how the flow of additional tourist expenditure is traced?
3. What is Ad-hoc multiplier? Build up a theoretical model of Ad-hoc multiplier after Archer.
4. Why the tourist multipliers vary from region to region?
5. Do you think Keynesian dynamic multiplier concept is applicable in tourism multiplier analysis? Justify your answer.
6. "While income effect of two types of tourist expenditure is almost same employment effect may be different"—explain the statement.
7. Find the values of tourist multiplier for both short run and long run with the following values:

The first round leakage out of the country = 0.7, marginal propensity to consume = 0.8, marginal propensity to import = 0.7, marginal rate of indirect taxation = 0.1, marginal rate of direct taxation = 0.2 and that of transfer payment = 0.2.

8. State whether the following statements are true or false.

   (*i*) Tourist multiplier is a unit free concept.

   (*ii*) Higher the marginal propensity to consume lower is the value of multiplier.

   (*iii*) Delphi modelling is a means of reaching consensus among experts.

   (*iv*) Input-Output approach is a general rather than partial approach of economic impact.

Chapter Six

Tourism and Environment

Few problems are as common to all countries regardless of economic system and level of development as environmental degradation. Economic (as well as tourism) activities rely on the use of natural resources and usually have significant effect on environment. But economic valuations in most cases stress more on short-term profit than long-term effects. The economic manifestations of environmental degradation are thus the most useful indicators for those who wish to pursue sustainable development.

With the phenomenal growth of tourism, comes the question of depletion of natural resources. Tourism and environment have an intimate relationship. In fact, environment is the resource base of tourism. It is the environment of a particular place, which attracts the tourists. The conservation of natural resources is therefore needed to sustain tourism. It is generally believed that tourism development activities rely on the use of natural resources and usually have significant effects on environment. But ecologists, soil scientists or natural system experts perform most of the environmental assessments. Very few studies are translated into the factors what can be evaluated in the same terms as economic variables. In this chapter the recent evolution of environmental economics is captured with special reference to some ecotourism studies.

The demand for outdoor recreation is growing as a consequence of increasing population, income and holiday entitlements. Some outdoor recreational activities are available as open access, non-priced goods. But, the problem exists on evaluating whether or not the benefits provided by the good exceed the costs of its provision and maintenance.

The gravitational characteristic of 'sun lust' demand implies disadvantage to many small third world countries for competitive capacities of some neighbouring nations as for example former Yugoslavia for Greece, Bulgaria for Turkey. Moreover, in many less developed countries international tourism is a highly concentrated phenomenon in terms of composition, direction and seasonality. Six western European countries dominated tourism in former Yugoslavia and 83 per cent of tourism took place during summer and mostly along Adriatic coast. Similarly, visitors to Turkey are mainly from northern Europe.

In many cases environmental considerations become important at the regional level where a range or spatial strategies are proposed to be implemented. In coastal sites prime objective is to avoid 'ribbon development'. Hence, the consideration on the fragile resources becomes important. Following the so-called 'honey-pot' strategy access may be given to another forest or camping site. A Contingent Valuation (CV) approach was applied to the problem of estimating recreation benefits from alleviating congestion at Indian Peaks wilderness area, Colorado of Canada. Random samples of 126 individuals were interviewed while hiking and backpacking in 1979 (Walsh and Gilliam, 1982). The results provide an empirical test and confirmation of the Cesario and Freeman proposals that under condition of excess recreational demand for existing sites, enhanced opportunities to substitute newly designated sites will reduce congestion and results in external benefits to the remaining peak day users.

In a locality like Digha (India) where such redirection is not possible for natural or geographical limitations, the planners are left with the task of restricting visitors to maintain the maximum carrying capacity.

Acceptable level of crowding appears to differ from one place to another. It is not place neutral. There cannot be any unique figure of crowding applicable both on a beach and at a hill station. Even the figure differs from beach to beach or hill to hill. While some studies observed 1000 persons per hectare or 10^2 metres per person as a measure of over crowding a beach, others estimate the magic figures as 15^2 metres per person considering the first 50 metres from the water edge (Pearce, 1981).

History of Growing Environmental Concern

The economic definition of non-renewable or exhaustible resource states that the inter-temporal sum of the services provided by a given stock of an exhaustible resource is finite. (Dasgupta and Heal, 1979). Hotelling in his classic paper (1931) defined the question of non-renewable resource use as that of allocating a given amount of resource stock in order to maximize the benefit from consuming that resource. The analysis of Hotelling was carried out using complicated mathematics, which deterred many economists of his time in understanding his ideas, although the basic economic logic was intuitive. During last 70 years the economic analysis of the question that Hotelling set rolling, gained momentum.

During second ASKO meeting held in 1994 at Stockholm, Sweden, Arrow, Costanza, Dasgupta, Maler, Perrings and others reported that National and International economic policy has usually ignored the environment. 'Economists', said Professor Amartya Sen, 'have by and large been more interested in analyzing objectives (e.g. in welfare economics) and technological relations (e.g. in studies of production function or of input output system) than on going into the thorny field of feasibility constraints' (Sen, 1980). Suppose, government wants to build a large tourist complex adjacent to the temple of Kedarnath in the Himalayas or core area of Kaziranga National Park and is prevented because of the non-availability of building materials. In this case, it is a technological limitation. If, on the other, materials are there, but people raise strong protest on the ground of religious sanctity, aesthetics or environment, then the limitation can be a feasibility constraint.

Ten years after Rachel Carson's account of the changes in the environment (Carson, 1962) an unofficial report commissioned by the Secretary-General of the United Nations Conference on the Human Environment (Ward and Dubos, 1972) paid the environmental attention to the economic development projects including tourism projects. The Organization of American States followed suit with a seminar on how to secure a lasting tourism (OAS, 1979). At that time the Club of Rome also drew attention to the limits of growth. The System Dynamics Group of MIT pointed out five crucial factors, viz., population growth, food production, industrialization, depletion of natural resources and pollution (Meadows *et al.*, 1972). Until the 1970s developing countries generally regarded environmental quality as a luxury that could be afforded only after they had attained a considerably higher level of economic development. However, with the advent of technology and industrialization and historical evolution of capitalism as a world order, the parameters defining development have changed.

Until the present day, Environmental Impact Assessment (EIA) was limited to the local impacts and at best regional impacts. Drawing attention to the global impacts of tourism Theuns argued that a comprehensive assessment of local, regional and global impacts of tourism might reveal that long-haul tourism is not sustainable because of the energy and the greenhouse gases, which are emitted (Theuns, 2001).

Sustainable economic valuations have therefore proved to be important tools in improving natural resource management and conservation. Sustainable development is development that meets the needs of the present without compromising the ability of future generations to meet their own needs. (World Commission on Environment and Development, 1987:43). The FAO simply describes sustainable development as being " A development which is environmentally non-degrading, technically appropriate, economically viable and socially acceptable" (Stephen, 1997). When the focus is on tourism, 'sustainable tourism' may be defined as 'the optimal use of natural and cultural resources for national development on an equitable and self-sustaining basis to provide a unique visitor experience and an improved quality of life through partnership among government, the private sector and communities' (OECD website, undated).

Nature-based Tourism, Ecotourism and Adventure Tourism

In the search of new tourism products, travellers and suppliers are today seeking to reshape the meaning of nature as a tourism attraction. Genuine non-urbanized nature—not just the whispering of the sea heard from a swimming-pool restaurant or skiing on well-maintained ski has emerged as a new attraction in the tourism market. New concepts and paradigms have been developed in order to guarantee the quality of a nature experience and to protect the natural and cultural bases for future businesses and generations of visitors.

On the heels of Industrial Revolution, western philosophy defined progress in material terms and measured development on a scale on a quantitative criteria. Ignoring resource capabilities of varying areas, the scale had an international hallmark. It ignored the necessity to consider climate differences or regional variations of mountains, plains or deserts. In the western nations this technological achievements of the Industrial Revolution led to unprecedented confidence in human superiority over controlling, combating and conquering nature. Neither in Adam Smith nor in Marx this so-called sustainable content was sufficiently addressed. Marx explicitly was of opinion that man changes nature and in course of that becomes "instruments of human domination of nature or of its activity in nature."

Thus, the need to plan in design with nature was shrugged off. 'Poetic justice', on the contrary throws greater scientific sense on nature's harmony as evidenced in Wordsworth, Tennyson or Tagore. Although Pigou (1920) applied the concept of externalities and social cost to environmental pollution, few economists discussed the relationship between human activity like outdoor recreation and environmental quality before 1960. Economists today are required to prove that the measurement of recreational demand is not a naive empirical trick.

Mainstream mass tourism, largely being urbanized sun-sand-sea tourism gradually becomes ethically, politically and ideologically intolerable. As Bryden puts it, 'whatever may be the economic benefits of mass tourism, their quantifiable and largely unquantifiable costs together are of sufficient weight to argue against further growth' (Bryden, 1973).

The deleterious economic effects of mass tourism are like leakages, misallocation of resources and creation of regional or enclave dualism. Leakages are expressed in high import contents of tourism. In countries like Caribbean Islands, Thailand and some far east islands import contents are ranging from 40 per cent to 60 per cent.

Soil erosion, deforestation and declining rainfall are some of the outcomes of ecological disorder caused by mass tourism. Acapulco of Mexico and many parts of Himalayas are classic examples where traffic concentration and housing establishments have destroyed the once heavily forested hills. Not only the hills, islands are also the soft targets in many cases. Bahamas with 180,000 resident population draws very little benefit from 1.5 million tourists. In areas like Tahiti, Philippines and Bermuda, high birth rates of illegitimate children were attributed to the carnival atmosphere generated by mass tourism.

The search for a substitute to the traditional mass-market tourism model culminated in the 1980s in the alternative tourism concept. This was demand—driven by travellers wishing to travel to the beaten tracks. Unfortunately these alternative travellers turned out to be the pioneers of mass tourism. Following the stage theories of tourism their ventures induced further tourists and thus the transitional phase turned them into mass tourism destinations.

From the devastating experience of mass tourism the ecotourism concept was developed in the late 1970s and unlike other alternative tourism it remains popular. It was based on the same criticism of mainstream tourism as that of alternative tourism, and more persistently recognized the environmental quality of unspoiled natural places as the main motive for some travel segments. Modern nature based tourism focuses on experiencing flora and fauna in natural settings. Trips to rain forest, whale watching, or encountering royal Bengal Tiger, all comes under the purview of modern nature based tourism. Today the term 'nature-tourism' is often used synonymously with 'ecotourism'.

Adventure tourism also falls into the category of nature-based tourism. As it involves the use of natural resources its purpose is to explore a new experience. It is usually connected to sports tourism and is exercised in forms of hiking, walking, mountain climbing, white water rafting or black water paddling, canyoning or kayaking. The growth of adventure tourism is also a reaction to sun and beach mass tourism. Modern travellers are fed up with holidays spent lazing away between deck chair, swimming pool and hotel bar and want to go after quite different holiday experiences.

The Association for Tourism and Leisure Education and the International Student Travel conducted an e-mail response survey of 2300 young travellers from eight origin countries on the long trips taken by young tourists (Mihalic, 2006). The study yielded a significant positive correlation between the motivations 'using physical skills', 'challenging my abilities' and 'searching for excitement'. The adventurers were likely to be more highly educated than other travellers, but there was no difference between the groups in terms of income.

Environmental Impact Assessment (EIA)

EIA has been addressed successfully by a range of valuation methods developed in environmental economics (Bishop, 1979; Smith and Crutila, 1982; Arrow *et al.*, 1993; Hadker *et al*, 1995; James and Murty, 1999; Chopra, 1997; Chattopadhyay and Mazumdar, 2001; Mitra and Chattopadhyay, 2002).

The economic value of environment needs to be specified in the background of three important features of environmental goods, namely *irreversibility, uncertainty and uniqueness* (Banerjee, 2001). Environment cannot be regenerated in a factory according to our wish or will. The old notion that we will first grow rich and then take care of environmental problems is an unacceptable proposition. In economic terms, path dependent equilibrium makes it very clear that it is often not possible to revert an old state of affair, once certain things have been destroyed and destroyed irreversibly. *Uncertainties* arise from our limited knowledge of the ecological balance. Lastly, many environmental or tourist attractions are *unique* in the sense their scenic beauties are not replicable. Relics of the historical past like Giza or Ajanta must have been built at great costs. Though theoretically possible, it would be almost impossible to build another Taj or Great Wall. Natural wanders like the Everest or Niagara are also unique to the fullest sense of the term.

EIA therefore appears to be synonymous with comprehensive or total economic valuation. In assessing total economic value of any extra market commodity like environment or tourist attraction three components of values are required to be estimated. These are *user value* (for those, who directly use the good and get benefit), *option value* (leaving the option open for future enjoyment by the same individual or future generation or general public) and *existence value* or *non-user value*. The existence value induces people to preserve the flora, fauna and natural resources. From this particular context any person, concerned with the theory of rationality has to come to terms with the narrow view of rationality.

Valuing the Non-Valuables—Travel Cost Method

Outdoor recreation being a form of extra market commodity has certain distinct characteristics that make it different from other products whose prices are determined through normal supply-demand interactions in the market. Since recreational and aesthetic experiences are not exchanged in a normal market, their valuation is very difficult. For a commodity like outdoor recreation, consumer is transported to the commodity for consumption to take place instead of vice versa. This is an advantage for statistical estimation or valuation. This is because the cost that is incurred for consumption (enjoyment) provides a surrogate price. Moreover, any investment in outdoor recreation (say, construction of roads) changes the price vector faced by the consumer (by reducing distance and there by travel time) at least to a section of consumers. Hence, to estimate environment we would want to describe this value in monetary term. The most widely adopted method of estimating environmental value relates to benefit rather than cost. Here the most popular method of estimating recreation value is called *Travel Cost Method* (TCM).

Hotelling originally proposed the travel coast approach in a letter to the US Department of Interior's National Park Service. It was later refined and applied by Clawson and Knetsch (1966). TCM involves using travel cost as a proxy for the value of visiting out door recreational sites. A statistical relation between observed visit and the cost of visiting is derived and used as surrogate demand curve. In this method the area around the recreation site is divided into a series of zones with equal travel costs. This may or may not be concentric zones. In the study of Arunachal Pradesh (Mitra and Chattopadhyay, 2003), zones were not assumed to be concentric but of various geographical regions.

Assuming all visits from the same zone have the same travel cost, people living in those zones are also assumed to be similar in respect to other factors. Data would then be collected from the visitors and the cost of the trip could be estimated. Next, the relationship between the cost of travel and the proportion of the population from each zone that visited the site is to be estimated. This produces the trip generating function. On the basis of the relationship shown in Figure 6.1 it is then possible to estimate the demand curve.

Individual travel cost model may be specified as:

$$V_{ij} = f(C_{ij}, S_{ij}, Y_{ij}, A_{ij}, H_{ij}, N_{ij})$$

Where

V_{ij} = number of visits made by individual *i* to site *j*
C_{ij} = individual *i*'s total cost of visiting site *j*
S_{ij} = individual's total cost in substitute destination of similar attraction
Y_{ij} = individual *i*'s household income
A_{ij} = age of individual *i*
H_{ij} = individual *i*'s household size
N_{ij} = size of individual *i*'s party.

Figure 6.1: Zones around a Recreation Site

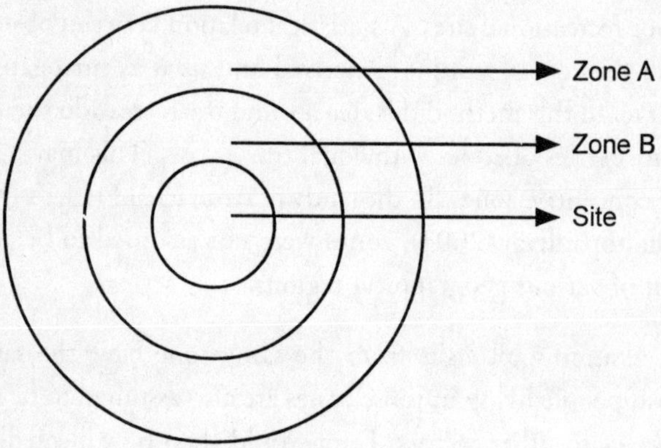

Although the approach had been developed and refined since it was first applied in late 1950s, limitations still remain. For instance, one issue, which trouble-researchers, is how to value the time, which people spend in travelling to the site. There are also problems with the visitors visiting many places of the site. Welzel (1977) showed that TCMs that fail to account for congestion produce underestimated recreation benefits at sites affected by congestion. Commenting of Wetzel's work, McConnell (1980) found that demand curves should be estimated with congestion held constant and that proper measurement of consumer surplus depended on correct sampling and specification of the demand function. Finally, the site may have many other values. Travel cost covers only part of the total value.

Figure 6.2: Relation between Travel Cost and Visitation Rate

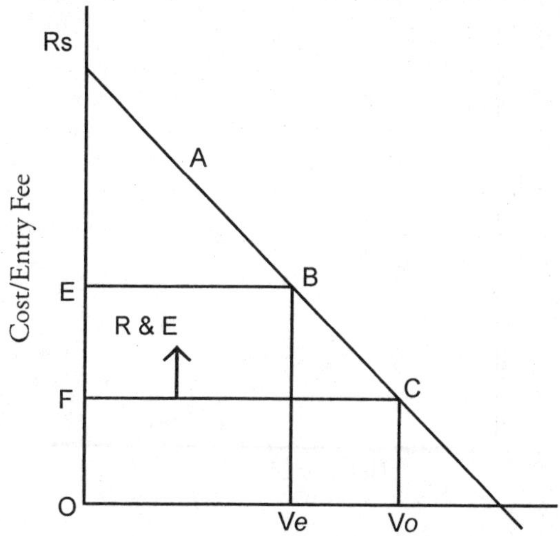

Visits per 1,000 Population per Year.

On the basis of relationship shown in Figure 6. 2, it is possible to estimate the demand curve for the site itself. The demand curve shows the relationship between price or in this case a hypothetical entry fee, and the quantity purchased, or in this case the number of visitors. The number of visitors is calculated for a range of different possible entry fees. It is here assumed that visitors would react to an entry fee in the same way that they would react to an increase in travel coasts. Thus, suppose that an entry fee of Rs. E was introduced. This would raise the total cost of visiting site Zone A from Rs. 0 to Rs. E, as shown in Figure 6.2. As a result number of visit would decline from V_0 to V*e* and the number can be estimated from the relationship in the figure. This calculation is then repeated from zone to zone and then repeated for a range of entry fees. From this, it is possible to calculate the demand curve as shown in Figure 6.3. The total area underneath the demand curve represents the value of the recreation site called *consumer surplus* where there is no entry fee. This also represents the total willingness to pay for the use of the site.

Figure 6.3: Demand Curve for the Recreation Site.

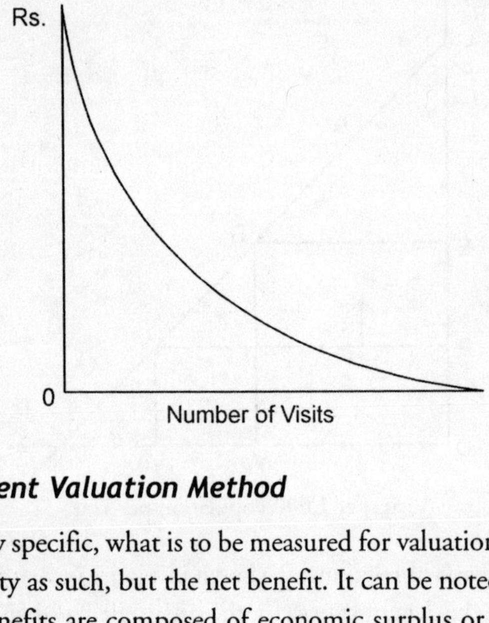

Contingent Valuation Method

To be very specific, what is to be measured for valuation is not the commodity as such, but the net benefit. It can be noted here that all net benefits are composed of economic surplus or producer's surplus (i.e. rent). Here we have two familiar tools of surplus measurement: Willingness To Pay (WTP) and Willingness To Sell (WTS). WTP is the maximum amount, the person is willing to pay to get a proposed change of environment. WTA is the minimum amount of compensation that would have to be paid to the affected individuals to make them well off, as they would be, if the change comes true.

However, the task of selecting the correct tool leads in many occasions to value judgement. If we dig down to the roots of benefit cost or welfare analysis, we will come to the Pareto Optimality condition and ultimately Kaldor-Hicks criterion. Pareto optimality condition states that a project will make the society better off if it leaves no individual of the society worse off but makes at least one person better off. This is to a large extent a limiting criterion since there is hardly any such project that does not make someone worse off. To this extent benefit cost analysis is more amenable to Kaldor-Hicks compensating criterion, which states that society is better off if the gainers completely compensate the losers.

Often the environmental impacts do not impose costs on firms, do not offer opportunities for averting behaviour and are not represented in the markets for particular goods. In this situation the most direct approach is simply to ask the affected people to give their estimate of the value involved. This technique based on expressed preferences is usually referred to as *Contingent Valuation Technique* (CVM).

Davis originally proposed the CVM in 1963. However, it was only after mid-seventies that the development of the method has gained proper momentum. This method is the most widely used and most controversial of all the environmental valuation techniques. Over past two decades CVM included estimates of the value of landscape, recreation, beaches, water quality, nature conservation, endangered species and so on.

Roughly speaking, it consists simply of asking individuals directly about the value they put on the amenity to be evaluated, that is their willingness to pay for it. However, doubts often hang over its results due, in particular to the hypothetical nature of the decision-making situation facing respondents.

Several biases highlighted in the literature of CVM affect the magnitudes of WTP and WTA. There is *information bias* when the respondents lack the information. The *strategic bias* occurs when the respondents know that their responses will affect the quality. *Starting point bias* leads the respondents to start with wrong amount of claimed compensation of payment. This arises due to insufficient knowledge or objectivity. Sometimes respondents try to impress the interviewer rather than state true WTP. This is called *warm glow* effect.

In spite of these limitations, thanks to *Blue Ribbon Panel's* recommendation the US Court has accepted CVM as the basis for assessing the damages. The incident behind this Blue Ribbon Panel is interesting—In 1989, the crud oil tanker Exxon Valdez ran around on the Reef in Prince William Sound, Alaska. Eleven million gallon of the total 50 million it was carrying poured into Sound, which caused massive devastation over 10,000 sq. mile area of water and 1,600 miles of shoreline. The oil killed about 2,650 sea otters. Over 20,000 dead birds were recovered including 100 bald eagles. Sound is important for commercial and recreational fishing and tourism. But there are non-use values like existence, option etc. In addition to legal action against Exxon Corporation and related companies a Contingent Valuation Study was commissioned. Conducting successful 1,043 interviews achieving a response rate of 75 per cent, the study came up with its report. If Exxon were found liable to be the damage caused, they would face an enormous bill for the non-use value alone. Hence, the analysis was at the centre of fierce debate. In this context the National Oceanic and Atmospheric Administration established a panel of distinguished economists including two Nobel laureates Arrow and Solow. The panel is known as *Blue Ribbon Panel.* The panel concluded that CVM could convey useful information that is sufficiently reliable for a starting point for the process of assessing damages in the court.

Empirical Illustrations

TCM and CVM were introduced in India for the first time by the middle of 1990s of the last century. As a matter of fact there were no applications of these techniques in the developing countries of Asia and the Pacific up to the 1980s. Indian Institute of Forest Management (IIFM) Bhopal did the first study of this type in India in early nineties on *Van Vihar* a reserve forest adjoining IIFM.

Then a group of researchers of Indira Gandhi Institute of Development Research (IIDS), Mumbai experimented the evidence from CVM of *Borivili National Park* (BNP), Mumbai (Hadker *et al.* (1995). Applicability and adaptability of the CVM, and the recommendations of the Blue Ribbon Panel, in the Indian context was tested. Methods to circumvent biases associated with the CVM were rigorously applied and discussed in the light of the evidence. The study also estimated the welfare measures from resource preservation.

Borivili National Park is the largest reserve located within the boundaries of a metropolis. It occupies a total land area of 103.09 sq. km accounting for a fifth of the Mumbai metropolitan region. More than 2.5 million people visit BNP annually making it the highest visited national park in the country. The study surveyed 134 respondents, though a small number as compared to the population of Mumbai yet. As predicted by the economic theory, the 'value' scale, the attitude index and the 'visit' scale were positively related to and were important determinants of the total WTP. To the question "are people willing to pay for BNP?" The authors found that the answer was an emphatic 'yes'. The study reported a true willingness to pay of Rs. 9.986 per household per month.

Chopra did the next important environmental study of nature-based recreation in 1997. She had applied a version of TCM to determine the value of tourism and the nature of the demand for it as part of her larger study on *Economic Valuation of Biodiversity: a case study of Keoldeo National Park, Bharatpur* (KNP*).* KNP is a 29 sq. km. mosaic of monsoon wetlands, seasonally flooded grasslands and thorny woodland. It is a designated world heritage site since 1985. It is a resting-place for many migratory birds including the Siberian Crane. Located within easy access from a number of other tourism sites, it has a very high tourism value. Data was collected regarding the tourist's travel and stay expense, duration of stay and various socio-economic characteristics.

The final set of usable responses consisted of 111 respondents, of whom 68 were Indians and 43 were foreigners. Demand function for tourism were set-up by making probability of visiting KNP to depend on (*i*) the amount spent on travel, (*ii*) opportunity cost of time (which in turn reflects household income), (*iii*) educational levels and (*iv*) reasons for visiting the park. Table 6.1 provides a summary of the costs and benefits arose out of KNP.

A forward-looking study on the inter linkage of environment and nature based tourism of Arunachal Pradesh was done during 2000-2002 (Mitra and Chattopadhyay, 2003). Following the TCM and Delphi technique the study provided economic estimates of recreational value of nature based tourism and also the economic potential for the development of such tourism in immensely nature-rich Arunachal Pradesh.

Arunachal Pradesh is a far-flung north-eastern Himalayan state of India with area 83,743-sq. km. and population of around 10.91 lakh as per 2001 census. Density of population of the state is lowest in India and it is around 13 persons per sq. km. Home of around 26 major tribes and 110 sub-tribes Arunachal is endowed with rich forest-based resources in green mountainous ranges, covering 81.92 per cent of the total geographical area as per the data based on satellite imagery in 1999. In around 2.5 per cent of India's land mass the state contains nearly 16 per cent of the total timber growing stock of the country.

During the survey altogether 309 effective interviews were conducted out of which 269 were domestic tourists and 40 foreign tourists. The tourists and the entrepreneurs providing tourist amenities were met at four tourist spots: Tawang, Bomdila, Namdapha and Ziro. The study observed that the visitation rate was clearly affected by local cost, age and education and annual household income were significant at 0.01 and 0.05 levels.

The paradox of tourism development is that the product needs to be consistently protected as it is being marketed. Unregulated tourism endangers and depletes the very resources and attributes that attract tourists. So it was felt necessary to relate both the aspects through TCM and Delphi. While the former yielded consumer surplus amounting to Rs. 991 per visit by Indian tourists and Rs. 1232 per visit by foreigners, the latter identified ten most significant negative impacts on environmental parameters. Table 6.2 gives an approximate estimate of the benefit received and cost incurred by different categories of the stakeholders considered.

Another interesting study on environmental valuation was done during same period in Calcutta (Chattopadhyay and Mazumder, 2001). The study brought out an ordered assimilation of various environmental issues and disorders relating to East Calcutta Wetlands (ECW). The study was based partly on empirical data and partly on Delphi type experts' opinion survey. It also used the CVM as its method in obtaining WTP.

Calcutta is a city of 14 million inhabitants. An area of wetlands of around 12,500 hectares marks the eastern fringes of the city. Recently Ramsar International has declared the site as Ramsar* site being the largest contiguous water body adjacent to a big city in the world. City Calcutta generates 1350 million litres of sewage a day. ECW take 70 per cent of this sewage through drainage channels and canals along with 3,000 metric tones of solid waste a day. These are used for fish cultivation and irrigation of vegetables growing plots. The whole recycling and recovery process provides direct employment for over 70,000 people and has a zero fossil fuel energy requirement. This tradition is now endangered. The wetlands are under threat of encroachment. During last 20 years the total area of ECW had been reduced to one third of its original area. Potential losses due to conversion of 1,500 hectares of ECW in the year 1999-2000 are shown in Table 6.3.

Sometimes both open ended question and dichotomous choice around a fixed payment are used on the same site and regression results are drawn separately as well as from pooled data. One such

---

* On 2 February, 1971, in the Iranian city of Ramsar, an important intergovernmental treaty on wetlands was adopted. It was the first of the modern global treaties on conservation and wise use of natural resources, and came to be popularly known as the "Ramsar Convention." While initially the Convention put emphasis on the habitat of water birds, over the years, the scope of the Convention broadened its scope to other wise use of wetlands. The Convention came into force in 1975 and has 133 contracting parties including India As of November, 2002 with 1201 wetland sites, totalling 105.8 million ha. designated for inclusion in the Ramsar List of Wetlands of International importance. Till November, 2006 were designates 25 wetlands as Ramsar Sites in India.

study was done in Hvar, Croatia. What can be concluded from general observation of all such studies is that WTP is strongly negatively correlated with length of stay and weakly negatively correlated to the age of respondent.

Many nature based tourism sites possess a lower standard of living than the region from which they draw their tourists. Changing values and attitude of host societies are therefore the most important outcomes of tourism. In many resorts the difference is overwhelming. Here, tourism should not inject the behaviour of wasteful society in the midst of a society of want (Boudhiba, 1976). No doubt mass tourism is the main cause of the breakdown of damaging environment. It literally drives the citizens out of town during peak seasons. Tiny Bermuda (24 sq. miles with 50,000 people) has set a ceiling of 450,000 arrivals. Tahiti, painter Gauguin's Paradise Isles with their free-loving, free-living people have become caricatures of his paintings.

In planning Eco-friendly tourism many developing countries are committing the same mistake what the developed world made earlier. Acapulco of Mexico where unplanned traffic concentration and housing estimates have destroyed the once heavily forested hillside. In Nepal 130,000 visitors shared the habitable third of 140,000 sq. km creating enormous hygienic—cum-environmental sufferings to this geographically handicapped country. Darjeeling, one of the finest hill resorts of world ranking beauty offers an excellent testing ground of various hypotheses current in the literature on the environmental impact of tourism.

Table 6.1
Benefit and Cost Flows from KNP during 1992-93
(Rs. Million at 92-93 Prices)

1. *Primary Benefits*	
Recreation benefits	8.950
Domestic nationals	7.791
Foreigners	1.159
Income from forest produces	0.057
Non-use value	40.886
Domestic nationals	25.173
Foreigners	15.713
2. *Secondary Benefits*	
Hotels and restaurants	1.160
Transporters	18.330
3. *Transfers*	
Visitor charges	2.126
Domestic nationals	0.261
Foreigners	0.793
Others	1.163
4. *Costs*	
Income losses to locals	18.330
Government investment expend.	3.895
Operating expenditures	2.25

Source: Murty and Menkhaus, 1994.

Table 6.2
Benefit and Cost Flows from Selected Tourist Spots of Arunachal Pradesh during 1999-2000
(Rs Lakh at 1999-2000 Prices)

1. *Primary Benefits*	
Recreation benefits	62.14
Domestic nationals	53.40
Foreigners	8.74

(*Contd.*)

2. *Secondary Benefits*	
Hotels and restaurants	43.06
Transporters	27.54
Employment to locals	53.54
3. *Transfer*	
Visitors charges	10.98
Domestic nationals	4.89
Foreigners	6.09
4. *Costs*	
Income losses to locals	54.45
Government investment expenditure	51.17
Operating expenditure	48.10

Table 6.3
Potential Losses due to Conversion of 1,500 Hectares of ECW 1999-2000

Type of Losses	*Value (Rs. in million)*
Revenue loss due to shrinkage in*	
(1) Paddy cultivation	87.00
(2) Pisciculture	14.15
(3) Medicinal plant	.10
Income loss due to shrinkage of indirect employment**	161.00
Loss of suspended solid	.87
Loss due to micro climatic instability #	3.78
Loss of non-use existence value	72.00
Total	338.90

Note: * These do not reflect income loss.

** Number of affected households 4751.

Single year annuity value.

Appendix

Sometimes to represent the probability of destination choice a binomial logit analysis is used. The analysis determines the parameters that can best describe the probability of selecting a destination as a function of different characteristics. The trade offs are measured between each characteristic and its money value (willingness to pay) through a hypothetical toll cost that was attributed to each destination scenario.

The binomial logit model is given by an equation that describes the probability that the *i*th respondent will choose the first alternative (W^1) over the second (W^2) as a function of the difference between quality characteristics and the money in tolls. For a single quality difference the model is given by:

Prob (W^1 is chosen by *i*) +

$$\frac{1}{\left[\ 1+e \quad [\beta_0^0 \ -{}^1\beta_0+\beta_q(q^0-q^1)+\beta_c(c^0-c^1)]\ \right]}$$

Where

$q^0 - q^1$ = Quality differences.

$c^0 - c^1$ = Toll difference (in Rs.).

and the parameters are estimated by a maximum likelihood estimation procedure using survey data.

To determine the willingness to pay for a destination characteristic change by the average individual, it is only necessary to find the amount of money that keeps the probability constant. That is, in order to balance the probability equation when destination quality changes from q^0 to q^1, the increase in cost would need to be:

$$-\frac{\beta_q}{\beta_c}(q^0 - q^1)$$

Thus, this can be interpreted as the individual's willingness to pay for a destination characteristic change from q^0 to q^1.

EXERCISES

1. What is extra market commodity? Give some examples of such commodities.
2. How Amartya Sen described feasibility constraint?
3. Show how Environmental Impact Assessment can be linked with total economic valuation?
4. Tick the correct answers of the followings:

   (*i*) Correlation between physical skills, and searching for excitement is very low / very high / zero.
   (*ii*) Acceptable level of crowding is place-neutral / not place-neutral.
   (*iii*) The notion that we will first grow rich and then take care of environmental problems is an unacceptable proposition / acceptable proposition.
   (*iv*) Travel Cost Approach was originally proposed by Pigou / Hotelling / Thunes.

5. Show how environment and tourism are intimately related to each other.
6. "National and International economic policies have usually ignored the environment." Do you share this view?

7. What is Blue Ribbon Panel?
8. What do you mean by sustainable development?
9. How sustainable tourism development can be linked with general sustainable development?
10. Distinguish between Travel Cost Method and Contingent Valuation Method (CVM).
11. Explain 'willingness to pay' and 'willingness to accept' in the context of CVM.
12. What are the biases one may encounter in following CVM?
13. What is Ramsar Site?

Chapter Seven

Tourism and Terrorism

Researches on tourism are mostly based on impact studies both actual and potential. That is, to quantify employment and income generated by tourist flow that has occurred or to be occurred at a particular tourist spot. But, very few studies are found where the emphasis is on the quantification of direct or indirect loss from not travelling to a destination.

This chapter examines the nature and extent of terrorism and its impact upon tourism. In contrast to traditional warfare, the covert nature of terrorism and the 'new war' suggests that increased civilian casualties and threats of bio-terrorism may leave few tourist markets.

Security Concerns on Tourism

Destination choice is a mental phenomenon on the part of a prospective traveller. Apart from attraction, accessibility and facility, the question of security emerges as an important determinant of tourism. Um and Crompton, (1992) captured this phenomenon in their study. They described the beliefs about a destination's attributes, which induce the visitors as "facilitators", and those attributes that are not congruent with a tourist's motive as "inhibitors." The authors suggested that the risk reducing inhibitor factors were likely to be deterministic rather than facilitators. Thus, tourist's perceptions of the safety of a destination become highly influential in decision-making.

Existence of social and political stability and absence of any kind of civil unrest are important pre-requisites for successful tourist trade. Terrorist incidents receiving media coverage have an almost immediate effect on the people, while it takes a long time to make people convinced about restoration of peace in an erstwhile-disturbed spot.

It has been observed that when some set of events dissuades tourists from visiting a given destination, the probability is that some other destination will benefit. For example, political disturbance in former Yugoslavia caused the shift of peak summer European market to elsewhere. Bali's market share increased at the cost of Fiji (Mc Donnell, 1996). Srilanka lost almost 10 per cent of international tourist arrivals between 1983 and 1989, while Maldives and India benefited at the cost of Srilanka (Gamage, 1997). Similar consequences are observed among the various regions of a single country. As for example, neighbouring state Himachal Pradesh skimmed the benefit of disturbed Kashmir (Chattopadhyay, 1998).

Most of the supply components of the tourist products are to a large extent within the control of the destination. Nevertheless, any concern over the security situation jeopardizes the demand for that destination.

Economic Intelligence Unit (1994) identified three categorical causes of disruption to international tourism: Fundamental long term disruption as has occurred in Lebanon, Northern Ireland, Srilanka, Uganda and former Yugoslavia. Continuing volatility in tourism destinations such as in Egypt, India, Israel, Philippines,

Turkey etc., and short-term single event disruption such as China, Fiji and Florida.

On many occasions tourists become incidental victims where most crimes are directed to the indigenous population. In some recent events some extremist organizations target tourists. A study on contribution of tourism to crime in the United States indicated that for five out of nine crimes, tourism was not found to be a determinant at all. For the remaining four, the magnitude could be considered insubstantial (Pizam, 1982). Beheading one Norwegian tourist and holding four others captive, battle hardened foreign militant groups like the *Al-Faran* with members from Afghanistan, Pakistan and even Sudan, brought a new dimension to the conflict in Kashmir Valley in 1995. In November, 1997, gunmen opened fire on tourists outside a 3,400-year-old temple in southern Egypt killing 60 tourists. In India, pilgrims to Amarnath and Vaishnodevi Caves, Raghunath and Swaminarayana Temples, have been targeted in recent years. Hence, protecting tourists from offenders is essential for the sustainable growth of tourism.

Seeds of Terrorism

Terrorism is an enigmatic and compelling phenomenon, which draws abundant intellectual attention. The often quoted cliché "one person's terrorist is another person's freedom fighter" succinctly portrays varying viewpoints and definitional problems. V.S Naipaul in his *Among the Believers—An Islamic Journey* echoed Bertrand Russell and remarked, 'Politics is combined with religion in Islam.' Nonetheless, it is difficult to subscribe the view that Islam as a faith is unable to reconcile the two extremities it sustained, namely liberalism and obscurantism. It is rather the extremists' version of Islam that is unable to harmonize. The renowned scholastic authority on Islam Professor Edwardsaid said that if this misbalance continued for long, a break point would be reached. One cannot say if that bubble burst happened on 11 September, 2001.

The terrorist attack on Israeli participants in Munich Olympic Games by the extremist outfit called *Black September* was the first major insurgency in the history of modern terrorism. World became familiar with the term "hijacking". The explosive myths of human bomb, suicide terrorism or *fidayeen* attack whatever be the brand reached its pinnacle in the event of September 11, 2001.

Two political declarations both under the supervision of the British can be singled out as being the subversive seeds of the present day's terrorism. These are Balfour Declaration and Instruments of Accession of Kashmir. The Balfour Declaration, which created Israel in 1947, was a British decision implemented by Winston Churchill. The latter was too a British decision and implemented by Lord Mountbatten in 1947. Very few do realize that in the process of relocating 250,000 Holocaust survivors, some 780,000 Palestinians were forced into UN refugee camps where most still live. The Middle East crisis dates to that event and smoldered into incidents like 9/11 and London Tube blasts. But unlike Middle East, Kashmir imbroglio is more a religious fascism than resource war over land and political hegemony.

Now-a-days, terrorist groups are almost microscopic. However, some major terrorist outfits are resorting to suicide terrorism in the name of Islam or simply for freedom of their homeland. The Liberation Tiger of Tamil Elam (LTTE) carried out the largest number of suicide attacks in its quest of statehood. It's the only group to claim two world leaders, Indian Prime Minister Rajiv Gandhi and Sri Lankan President Ranasinghe Premadasa.

Hizbollah of Lebanon is second to the LTTE. Next comes the most subversive and lethal group called Al-Qaida headed by Osama bin Laden and Ayman al-Zawahiri. Both of them have come from privileged background. Al-Qaida is the prime suspect of 11/9 attack of New York and Washington. Their focus is almost single minded- the US (Great Satan) and Israel (Little Satan) and their allies including India.

Hamas stands fourth in suicide attack. This group is active in Gaza and West Bank and has vowed to destroy the Zionist State Israel. Kurdistan Workers Party stands fifth in this order. Several other groups include *Lashkar-e-Toiba* and *Jaish-e-Mohammed*, both headquartered in Pakistan has links with Osama and also profess a radical Pan-Islamism of the Al-Qaida variety.

The World Tourism Organization (WTO) blamed the threat of terrorism, for $105 billion lost (unearned) tourism receipts in 1985. Mediterranean countries suffered when bookings declined by 50 per cent during the same period and bookings dropped 65 per cent in Egypt when American visitors cancelled their plans. Terrorism is a global phenomenon today. The most subversive testimony being the 11/9 attacks on the twin towers of New York and Pentagon Headquarters of Washington in 2001. International tourism was never so hard hit as it was in 2001-02. Between 1972-1988 and 1993-96, fifty-two terrorist incidents had been identified by a joint study of the State Universities of Arizona and Pennsylvania where tourists were the prime targets. Egypt, the citadel of world's ancient civilization was found to be the epicenter of international terrorism. Six international tourists, who were taken hostage in Kashmir by a militant group where one escaped and one was decapitated, made India's entry in this unpleasant league.

Of late, terrorism in Kashmir has found a very strong peer case in Chechnya. Geographical area of Chechnya and Kashmir Valley is nearly same. Chechnya has just approximately 17,000 sq. km of territory after it was separated from Ingushetiya. For most people it is difficult to locate Chechnya and the Indian part of Kashmir Valley in the world map. The juxtaposition of comparative demographic data is still more revealing. Russia has a population of 146 million while Chechnya has just 8.5 lakh people. That is less than one per cent. Of them according to the western sources three lakh Russians or Russian speaking population had fled the war ravaged Chechnya.

Kashmir Valley on the other has an area of about 16,000 sq. km after the armistice was declared in 1947. Jammu and Kashmir has a population of around ten million while Kashmir Valley has just five million people. Here too, about three lakhs of Hindu Kashmiris had left the Valley. In both these places (Kashmir and Chechnya) roots of the violence are not purely ethnic, not necessarily Islamic and certainly not entirely territorial.

One may deduct the refugee figures, females, children and senior citizens from the total population. In that case the able-bodied male citizens are supposed to be susceptible to terrorism. What is surprising in Chechnya, all the able-bodied male citizens are not necessarily gun-wielding fighters? The tragedy shows a significant graphic tally. In Chechnya the Militants killed 242 people in a span of only 10 months period (i.e. October, 2002 to August, 2003). In Jammu and Kashmir the figure was 357 in six years (from January, 1997 to July, 2003).

History of terrorism in Chechnya is comparatively of recent origin. The Russian Information Agency had reported that between 1995-99, more than 1,700 people were kidnapped and unofficial figures have pegged it at 2000. In a single post-Soviet year 1991-92 some 1200 murders took place in Chechnya.

Financing terrorism in Chechnya and Kashmir is not of identical nature. In 1993-94 alone Chechen bandits had accumulated some $ 4 million from train raids in the north Caucasian line. Criminal groups undertook production of counterfeit currency. In October, 1999 Russian police detained 90 Chechens and confiscated from them 5,98,000 false dollars. In India, Kashmir terrorism is mostly funded by foreign sources.

Terrorism based on Islamic fundamentalism is not only a menace to the countries like India, Israel or Egypt. This has become a matter of grave concern to the countries like Philippines or China. Concern over the three *isms*—terrorism, extremism and separatism—is one of the main reasons why the Chinese have taken the initiative of establishing Shanghai Cooperation Organization by roping in Russia, Kazakhstan, Uzbekistan, Kyrgyzstan and Tajikistan. In short, it is known as *Shanghai Six* inclusive China.

Islam is not normally associated with China, as it is with India or Indonesia. Beginning in the 10th century Muslim traders played an important role in globalizing China's economy. They filled the gap caused by the demise of Indian Buddhism and promoted Sino-Indian trade. The famous Chinese explorer Admiral Zheng He, who made several epochal voyages in the first-two decades of the 15th century, including some to the Malaber Coast, was a Muslim.

As late as during the Cultural Revolution, the *Weizhou* Great Mosque in northern China, described as the most beautiful mosque in China, was destroyed. During early eighties the Muslims started to get increasing political, economic and cultural space. Muslim students indulged in public protests in 1989 for instance, against the publication of a book in Chinese called Xing Fengsu (Sexual Customs).

It has been estimated that today about two per cent of Chinese is Muslim. Xinjiang has been a Muslim dominated province but in typical Chinese style, the demographics have been altered (as was the case in Tibet) by the mass settlement of the dominant Han communities. Over the past four decades Han proportion of the

Xinjiang's population increased to at least 40 per cent. Xinjiang's importance lies in its natural resources like hydrocarbons and minerals. The area of the province covers one sixth of the total land of China. This Xinjiang Uygur Autonomous Region is called the 'Kashmir of China'. Economically backward in this region income inequality is extremely high. Considering the mineral resources the region can be compared with Bihar of India. While per capita income of China is $750, for Xinjiang this is only $187 in 1989.

The Uygur of Xinjiang are one of the 10 so-called Muslim nationalities of China, the others being the Hui, Kazak, Dongxiang, Kyrgyz, Salar, Tajik, Uzbek, Baoan and Tatar. The Hui are the most numerous and found all over China especially Ningxia, Gansu, Henan, Xinjiang, Quinghai, Yunan and Hob. In recent years, particularly after partial lifting of embargo on inter-state migration, millions of citizens have migrated from Gansu to neighbouring provinces in search of job and making fortune. A bloody riot took place in Yinning on 5 February, 1997. Many had died when Uygurs organized street protests demanding independence. The western media reported that in 1998, the strong 5,00,000 People's Army crushed the riot ruthlessly.

Cost of Terrorism and New War

September 11, 2001 (9/11) has been described as a 'watershed' in world history (Zakaria, 2001) of terrorism. It was the first attack on the American mainland by a foreign adversary since the war of 1812. The Milkin Institute (Navarro and Spencer, 2001) assessed the immediate costs to the USA, including: (1) the physical damage to US property as at least US 10 billion; lost economic output in the immediate further aftermath (including diminished airline and hotel revenues and reduced consumer spending) at $ 47 billion;

and (3) the costs for "terrorist tax" (security) as upto US $ 41 billion. The estimated total price tag approaches US $ 2 trillion.

The fear factor caused by 9/11 engulfed the stock market of both Europe and Asia, and also spread to the hotel and restaurant industry. The global economic loss of tourism revenues is incalculable, but the impacts were evident worldwide: two national European airlines (Sabana and Swiss Air) declared bankruptcy, and literally thousands of US travel agencies went out of business. The lost tourist jobs were critical to many international destinations.

Kashmir Imbroglio

The Kashmir Valley is a part of the mountainous region lying between the Karakoram in the North and the Pir Panjal range of the Himalayas in the South and Southwest. The bean-shaped valley of Kashmir in the Himalayas is one of the most picturesque valleys in the world situated between 33 degree Latitudes and 34 degree Latitudes North and 76 degree Longitudes and 74 degree Longitudes East in the northern region of India. The valley is more or less flat at an average altitude of 1500 metres above sea level. It measures about 140 km in length from Southeast to Northeast, while its width varies from 30 km to 40 km. The area is approximately 5,300 sq. km.

As a tourist destination Jammu and Kashmir is twice blessed. First, there are plenty of tourist attractions including fascinating trekking routes, holy shrines, lofty hills or captivating wild life. On the other, there are innumerable buyers both domestic and international. The only problems lying here are infrastructure and violence. Since independence, this Heavenly State fell victim caused by ever-growing stock piling on the part of both India and Pakistan. The total military spending jointly by India and Pakistan is one of the highest among the countries of the world. The celebrated economist of Pakistan late Mehbub-ul-Haque analyzed in great detail the potential peace dividend of both Pakistan and India. Even a minuscule of this amount is bound to bring handsome dividend for tourism industry in Kashmir.

Table 7.1
Terrorists and Civilians Killed in J&K
(Upto 31 July, 2003)

Year	Total terrorists killed	Foreign terrorists killed	Total civilian killed	Total killed
1990	550	0	461	1011
1991	844	2	382	1226
1992	819	0	634	1453
1993	1310	79	747	2057
1994	1596	77	820	2416
1995	1332	77	1031	2363
1996	1209	213	1336	2545
1997	1075	260	948	2023
1998	999	406	857	1856
1999	1082	548	821	1903
2000	1612	870	762	2374
2001	2020	1198	919	2939
2002	1707	1063	922	2629
2003	793	394	466	1259
Total	16948	5193	11106	28054

Source: www.armyinkashmir.org/militant.htmail.

What is happening in Kashmir today is a human tragedy. Since the eighties of last century, a latent secessionism, turned into a full-blown movement called *azadi* (liberation) as well as a conflict between militant Moslems and peaceful miniscule Hindus. Thousands have died, normal lives have been disrupted and the economy is in shamble. As a result tourism the most dominant and viable sector of the local economy has been crippled for over a decade. During nineties Kashmir had lost about ten million tourists.

The loss in terms of foreign exchange was approximately $1 billion. Average annual loss of employment in this sector was around 2,00,000 (Chattopadhyay, 1998).

The figure on killings in Jammu and Kashmir used here is based on the official Indian Army source. Hence unofficial figures might be much higher.

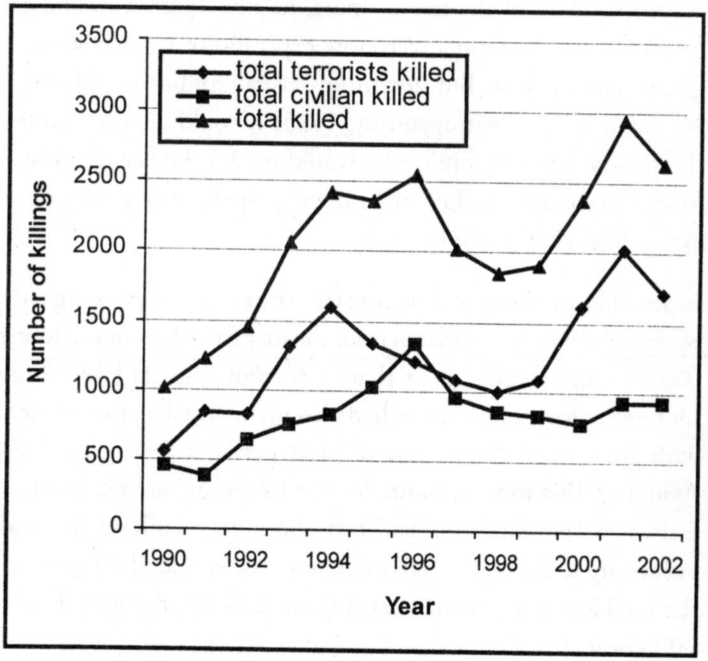

Figure 7.1: Killings in Kashmir.

Tourist reaction to terrorism can best be understood from a single year's figure of 1990. While five-lakh visitors visited Kashmir Valley in 1989, the number sharply came down to only ten thousand the next year. It is surprising to note that domestic tourists were more susceptible to the disturbances than their foreign counter parts. Even during the bleak years of the decade, when the number of domestic visitors to the valley was on the wane at an increasing rate, foreign visitors had maintained a slightly increasing trend, though it never reached its peak previous level of 1989.

As observed from different studies, average length of stay of a foreign tourist in India is normally 26 days. In Kashmir their stay is little over 10 days. The loss of direct foreign exchange earning throughout nineties had been estimated to about $ 700 million.

In a country of the size of India, it is not easy to estimate in precise terms the inputs of tourist expenditure in each sector of goods and services. But accepting several studies (IIPO, 1972; NCAER, 1975; Chattopadhyay, 1995) it could be assumed that the resultant tourist multiplier would be 2.5. Hence, the loss of foreign exchange would further deprive the local economy to the extent of $ 1750 million.

In the domain of domestic tourism, loss is equally overwhelming. In normal period, the number of domestic tourist was 11 times higher than that of foreign tourists in Kashmir. Domestic flow to the valley had also maintained a positive trend with an average annual rate of three per cent during 1980-88. Assuming this modest figure for the following years it had been estimated that Kashmir had lost about 10.6 million domestic visitors up to 2002. With five days stay and standard expenditure, the total lost direct tourist earning could be approximated to Rs. 20 billion.

Study on Srilanka suggested that each 12 additional visitors in Srilanka generate one direct job (Gamage *et al.*, 1997). Though this inference is region specific it gives some idea about using this tourist-employment ratio as a proxy measure. Detail estimates made in many countries show that indirect employment induced by tourism is generally higher than direct employment. Certain estimates show that it is twice as much as indirect employment as direct employment (Chib, 1981). As a conservative estimate, the tourism sector thus generated total employment of about 45,000 in the beginning of nineties of last century in Jammu and Kashmir.

Political unrest and terrorism almost destroyed the tourism industry in the Kashmir Valley for over a decade. During past 50 years, a sea change has taken place not only in people's standard of living but also in their value system and attitude towards enjoyment of leisure among the Indian middle class. The latent change in the level of income and purchasing power cum pattern has not been estimated quantitatively in the light of tourism demand so far. Susceptibility of the demand for tourism to this growth of income has been established empirically for various countries. In some studies, it was found that one per cent rise in real income results in 1.5 to 1.8 times increase in propensity to travel.

In many affluent societies, tourism enjoys the highest preference in the use of supernumerary income. A new generation of tourist is thus emerging very fast in the process of growth of consumer society. The number of Indians participating in this 'consumer boom' is estimated to 100 million. Most of them live in cities. Another 200 million rich farmers and other people live in the villages. A sizeable portion of this potent stock fails to head for its very own *Paradise* due to the persistent trouble in the Valley.

EXERCISES

1. 'Destination choice is a mental phenomenon on the part of a prospective traveller.'—explain the statement.
2. Mention some important incidents of terrorist attack that influenced the tourists' visit adversely.
3. What are the two subversive seeds of the present day's terrorism?

4. What are the similarities and dissimilarities of terrorism in Kashmir and Chechnya?
5. What is *Shanghai Six?*
6. "September 11, 2001 (9/11) has been described as a 'watershed' in world history", explain.

Chapter Eight

Conclusion

In 1841, the train that rolled out of Leicester station carrying 570 vacationers with one Mr. Thomas Cook as tour guide opened a truly unique chapter in travel and tourism. Subsequently his first organized tour of the continent in 1856 ushered in an era in international tourism. Every year, a wave of tourists started to descend on the Mediterranean from Northern Europe, especially Scandinavian region. They rushed on to the Caribbean and even to the northern part of Africa. With the beginning of the eighties, this pleasure periphery has been extended towards South Asia, and the Far East. Now-a-days, one single global periphery is emerging. Today one can find German tourists in Goa, Japanese honeymooners in Guam, French vacationers in Vanuatu or American travellers in South Africa.

Many authors believe that in years to come, the vexing question will be not to organize work but leisure (Becker, 1965; Burton, 1971; Cohen, 1973). Apart from leisure, the rise in literacy and educational standard, better healthcare, communication development and increase in discretionary income in real term (partly due to double income families with fewer children) are some of the forces behind this growth of modern tourism.

As observed from the study while trend of tourist arrivals is marked by a rising trend, it is highly unbalanced among the regions. The bulk of tourism business is concentrated in Europe and North America. When the comparison is made between selected countries of South Asia, it is observed that India's share in international tourist arrival is the lowest (Kumar, 1997). India's share in world tourist arrival is a meager 0.40 per cent, insignificant compared to many smaller countries. Austria, a country of barely 12 million people attracts tourist inflow of over 19 million each year. Countries like Malaysia, Singapore or Thailand who cannot offer even half the diverse tourist attractions of India, have found their place in the list of world's top 20 tourism destinations. India failed.

One common content of most of the recent studies on Indian tourism is that the country has not been sold as a holiday destination and recreation. In Srilanka, the official statistics reveal that the main motivation of 91 per cent visitors is pleasure. Pleasure tourism mainly consists of beach holidays there. But Indian resorts receive number of visitors which is much below the total carrying capacity of the resorts in spite of being less expensive and close to nature character. Some authors wonder if India has missed holiday tourism simply because its planning strategy and developmental procedures have been too slow and inadequate or whether there is too fundamental reason, an unconscious aversion to pleasure rooted in puritanical ethic (Chib, 1981). Some find damaging impact of tourism with spectacle of thousands lying on the sunny beaches wearing just a fig leaf. In fact, it is difficult to judge if it is more jeopardizing morally than the press coverage of Madonna affair or sex violence in Hollywood movies.

In little over a decade, India has become one of the significant emerging economies. Its economy is growing at over 8 per cent a year, making it the fastest growing free market democracy. Indian industry is ticking along at double digit, while service sector continues to lead the overall growth surge. It is tourism however, which has recorded the highest levels of growth- more than 15 per cent per annum over the last three years. A recent study by NCAER reveals that tourism's contribution towards GDP (both direct and indirect) is 5.9 per cent, and towards employment (both direct and indirect) 8.78 per cent.

Opening up of the skies and a successful branding and positioning campaign 'Incredible India' have driven the growth of tourism in India. According to the International Civil Aviation Organization, every $100 of output produced and every 100 jobs generated by air transport trigger additional demand of $325 and 610 jobs in other industries throughout the global economy. Restrictive civil aviation policies had hitherto led to a loss in terms of business, employment and tourism. The new policy initiatives have led to the emergence of low cost carriers for the benefit of consumers. As a consequence, during the Tenth Plan period tourist arrivals grew by 78 per cent, while foreign exchange earnings increased by 122 per cent.

In the context of changing cultural scenario, one must realize the great sociological change that is taking place across the globe. The changing Islamic world may be an interesting case in point. Neglect of seacoast in Lebanon in particular and throughout the Islamic world in general is the result of the differences in attitude towards what is attractive. Now-a-days countries belonging to the Islamic faith being richly gifted with fascinating beaches are getting more and more convinced with enormous potential stored in tourism. In countries like Libya, Morocco, Tunisia, Egypt, Albania, Malaysia or Indonesia tourism is coming of age with great promise.

Very recently alternative tourism is catching on fast. Thailand is creating 'exercise centres' for health buffs and retirement villages for western pensioners sick of the crowds and the high prices in Florida or Cot d Azur. Bali is building huge conference centres in the hope of becoming the 'Geneva of the East'. Tours are proliferating that cater bird watchers, theatre and music lovers, golfers, scuba divers, surfers and lovers of endangered species. In Rwanda, foreigners pay about $200 per person for an hour's viewing of Mountain Gorillas in the 'Parc National de Volcanoes'. Each lion in Kenya's National Park attracts visitors worth 27,000 per year. A recent addition to this alternative tourism is 'health tourism'. In India the industry estimated that in 2005 there were 1,50,000 foreign visitors to hospitals.

According to a joint survey by the Confederation of Indian Industries and management consultancy firm McKinsey; medical tourism will become a $2-billion business by 2012. The comparative advantage in cost of treatment of India can be estimated from Table 8.1.

Table 8.1
Estimates of Cost of Treatment in the US and India

Type of treatment	*US ($)*	*India ($)*
Bone marrow transplant	400,000	30,000
Open heart surgery	50,000	4,400
Neurosurgery	29,000	8,000
Knee surgery	16,000	4,500
Lever transplant	500,000	40,000

Source: CII, 2005.

In the alarming growth of India's trade deficit, it is worthy to be noted that tourism registered an average annual growth of about six per cent during past 50 years. This has been achieved in spite of getting lower priority in the plan outlays (Chattopadhyay, 1995). With four billion foreign exchange earning and three million international travels, tourism is one of the largest foreign exchange earners with least leakage factor. India was the first country in Asia to recognize the potential of tourism and opened tourist offices in early fifties in Europe. But, the strong inward looking policies failed to reap the benefit of international tourism in spite of having strong English speaking legacy and liberal democracy. The situation has however, been changing in recent years.

In this context, China's performance is worth mentioning. China receives about 40 million inbound international tourists excluding ethnic Chinese compatriots from Hong Kong, Taiwan and Macao. This puts China in fourth position after France, the United States and Spain among the world's leading tourist destinations. As per WTO forecasting, in 2020 China would be the top inbound destination and the fourth largest outbound tourist generating market. After prolonged Communist isolation China is opening its frontiers to the overseas visitors and continues to accord tourism great importance. Olympic 2008 would no doubt be a great leap forward to this end.

Picture of ethnic Indian compatriots is no less gloomy. The NRI's are a sizable lot and most of them are quite well off. In the US, as reported in one of the AT&T bulletins, the Indians are the richest ethnic group. According to data released by World Bank India tops remittance list in the World. NRIs sent back over $25.7 billion in 2006. In the major 25 countries, in whose currencies India is interested, the size of the NRIs provides a tremendous potentiality for the tourism sector in India. India also has a middle class, bigger in size than the combined population of all the OECD countries of Europe. A new generation tourist is emerging very fast in the process of growth of this consumer society. Not only the trekking and hiking wave is inducing the new generation youth to travel, the scenario of tourism culture is taking a new shape with increased popularity of holiday homes and beach tourism. At present India sends more tourists abroad than it receives. The Country experienced a fantastic growth in the number of domestic tourism. In 2006 more than 420 million Indians travelled within the country staying in hotels alone. The figure was 236 million four years ago. Many more stayed in other places like guest houses, holiday homes, tents, and relatives' residences.

India and China are two growing economic powers as well as emerging powerhouses in outbound tourism too. WTO expected China's outbound travellers to number 100 million in 2005. India's could be of the order of 50 million with the business going at 25 per cent per year over the previous year. Some authors suggest a figure of two million tourists each way between India and China during same period. Assuming a modest expenditure of $500 per visitor this means additional foreign exchange earning of $1 billion for each country at the very least. This is one-third of India's current tourist earning and one seventh of China's.

In spite of being a late starter in international tourism China surged much ahead of India in terms of both number of incoming visitors as well as in foreign exchange earning. But unlike India Chinese tourism is concentrated to its nine coastal provinces and three municipalities only. The provinces are: Liaoning, Hebei, Shandong, Jiangsu, Zhejiang, Fujian, Guandong Guangxi and Hainan. The municipalities are Beijing, Tianjin and Shanghai. These coastal regions obtain most of China's tourism receipts (90%) and account for most of China's tourist arrivals (84%) (Wen and Tisdell, 1996). This area is also rich in human resources and technological capabilities with high levels of productivity, high living standards and a rapid rate of capital accumulation. The supply side indicators also reveal a bias of tourism in favour of coastal areas though the bias is less marked than for demand side factors.

CONCLUSION

In India spatial inequality in the distribution of inbound tourism is not so pronounced. As sea on three sides and the Himalayas on the north surround the country, tourist attractions are well-distributed. In other words, the country is more or less evenly blessed with tourist attractions. Apart from capital Delhi, three presidential cities Mumbai, Chennai and Kolkata along with Bangalore, Tiruvanatapuram and Goa are major entry points of inbound tourists in India. In China the heavy concentration of tourism on the coastal areas and their higher economic gains from tourism mean that inland areas are less able to profit from their rich tourism resources. In India plenty of inland areas far from big industrial centres are there where tourism is the major propelling force in local as well as regional economy. Ajanta-Ellora, Khajuraho, Halebid-Belur, Tirupati, Ooti, Vaishnodevi and various Himalayan stations are some such examples.

Bibliography

Anderson, R.I., Fok, R. and Scott, J. (2000). *Hotel Industry Efficiency: An Advanced Linear Programming Examination.* American Business Review, January 40-48.

Archer, B. (1973). *The Impact of Domestic Tourism*, University of Wales Press, Cardiff.

Archer, B. (1976). *The Anatomy of a Multiplier*, Regional Studies 10 (71-77).

Archer, B. (1977). *Tourism Multipliers: The State of the Art*, University of Wales Press, Cardiff.

Archer, B. and Owen, C. (1971). *Towards a Tourist Regional Multiplier Regional Studies* 5 (289-294).

Archer, B. and Fletcher, J. (1990). *Multiplier Analysis in Tourism*, University of Surrey.

Archer, B.H. (1979). *Tourism in Carlisle and Kendal: A Report Prepared for Cumbria Tourist Board and Cumbria County Council.* Department of Hotel, Catering and Tourism Management, University of Surrey, Guildford, Surrey, England.

Armstrong (1972). *International Tourism—Coming or Going*, Future, Jun, 1972.

BIBLIOGRAPHY

Arrow, K. (1976). *Planning for Tourism Development—Quantitative Approach*, Preager Publishers, New York, N Y.

Arrow, K.B. Bolin, Costanza, R. Dasgupta, P. Folke, C. Holling, C.H., B-O. Jansson, S. Levin, K.G. Maler, C. Perrings, and Pimentel, D. (1995). *Economic Growth, Carrying Capacity, and the Environment, Science,* Vol. 268.

Arrow, K.R., Solow and others, (1993). *Report on the National Oceanic and Atmospheric* (NOAA), Panel on Contingency Valuation (Washington DC Resource for future).

Bagehot, W. (1882). *Lombard Street, London 1882.* Quoted in A.U. Wright (1956).

Balassa, B. (1964). *The Purchasing Power Parity Doctrine: A Reappraisal,* Journal of Political Economy, December

Banerjee, Sharmila (2001). *Economic Valuation of Environmental Benefits and Costs, Environmental Economics an Indian Perspective* Ed. R.N. Bhattacharya, Oxford University Press, New Delhi.

Banker, R.D. and R.C. Morey (1986). *Efficiency Analysis for Exogenously Fixed Inputs and Outputs,* Operations Research, 34(4), 513-521.

Becker, Gary S. (1965). *A Theory of the Allocation of Time,* The Economic Journal 75 (299).

Bell, R.A. and R.C. Morey, (1995), *Increasing the Efficiency of Corporate Travel Management through Macro Benchmarking,* Journal of Travel Research 33(3) 11-21.

Bhagwati, J. (1984). *Why Are Services Cheaper in Poor Countries?* Economic Journal 94.

Bishop, R.C. (1979). *Valuation of Extra Market Goods: Potential Applications of Travel Cost and Hypothetical Methods in Asia and the Pacific Basin.* Economic Approaches to Natural Resources and Environmental Quality Analysis, Eds. M.M Hufschmidt and E.L. Hyman Dublin.

Blake, C. and S. Mc Dowall, (1967). *A Local Input-Output Table,* Scottish Journal of Political Economy 14(227-242).

Boserup, M. (1969). *A Note on the Pre-History of Kahn Multiplier,* Economic Journal 79(667-669).

Bosetti, V.; M. Cassinelli and A. Lanza (2002). *The Economics of Tourism and Sustainable Development,* Ed. A Lanza, Edward Elger.

Boudhiba, Abdelwaheb, (1976). *The Impact of Tourism on Traditional Values and Beliefs in Tunisia,* Paper presented to joint UNESCO-World Bank Seminar on the Social and Cultural Impacts of Tourism Washington DC, December 8-10.

Brownrigg M. and M.A. Greig (1975). *Differential Multipliers for Tourism,* Scottish Journal of Political Economy, 22(3).

Bryden, J.M. (1973). *Tourism and Development—A Case Study of Commonwealth Caribbean,* Cambridge University Press, NY.

Burton, Thomas I. (1971). *Experiments in Recreation Research London,* George Allen and Unwin.

Carson, Rachel (1962). *Silent Spring.* Greenwich Conn., Fawcett Publications.

Cesario, F.J. (1980). *Congestion and Valuation of Recreation Benefits,* Land Economics, 56: 329-38.

Chattopadhyay, K. and C. Neogi (2004). *Economic Impact of Tourism Development—A Linear Programming Approach, In Tourism Management—The Socio-Economic and Ecological Perspective,* Eds. Panda, Misra and Parida, Universities Press, Calcutta.

Chattopadhyay, K. and K. Mazumder (2002). *Economics of Environmental Degradation, the Case of East Kolkata Wetlands. In* Kolkata the City of Wetlands. Mukherjee, M. and K. Chattopadhyay Ed. Government of West Bengal.

Chattopadhyay, K. (1993). *Hunting in Other People's Forest—Some Environmental Issues of Tourism Journal of Human Ecology,* New Delhi.

Chattopadhyay, K. (1995). *From Xenophobia to Globalization—Some Key Issues,* Finance India, IX (2).

Chattopadhyay, K. (1995). *Economic Impact of Tourism Development: An Indian Experience.* Kanishka, Delhi.

Chattopadhyay, K. (1995). *International Tourism Demand for India,* Artha Vijnana, XXXVII (2).

Chattopadhyay, K. (1998). *Cost of Terrorism to Tourism in Kashmir,* Dept. of Economics and Statistics, Government of Jammu and Kashmir.

Chattopadhyay, K. (1998). *Marketing Tourism Product—A Consumer Travel Decision Approach,* The Asian Economic Review, XL (2).

Chattopadhyay, M.R. Mukherjee and A. Rudra (1989). *Inter and Intra Occupational Differences in Income and Level of Living,* Economic and Political Weekly, 24 (16), Bombay.

Chib, S.N. (1981). *Perspective on Tourism in India,* Ministry of Information and Broadcasting, Government of India.

Chopra, K. (1997). *Economic Valuation of Biodiversity.* Institute of Economic Growth, Delhi.

Cisario, F.J. (1969). *Operation Research in Outdoor Recreation,* Journal of Leisure Research, 1(1), Winter.

Clark, J.M. (1943). *Studies in the Economics of Overhead Costs,* Chicago University Press, Illinois.

Clawson, M. and J.L. Knetsch (1966). *Economics of Outdoor Recreation,* Baltimore Johns Hopkins University Press.

Cohen, E. (1978). *Impact of Tourism on the Physical Environment,* ATR 5 (2).

Cohen, Erik (1973). *Nomads from Affluence: Notes on the Phenomenon of Drifter Tourism,* International Journal of Comparative Sociology 14 (1-2).

Darden, W.R. and W.J. Perreault (1975). *A Multivariate Analysis of Media Exposures and Vacation Behaviour with Life Cycle Covariates.* Journal of Consumer Research, September.

Dasgupta, P.S and G.M. Heal (1979). *The Economic Theory and Exhaustible Resources,* Cambridge University Press.

Diamond, J. (1977). *Tourism's Role in Economic Development—The Case Reexamined,* Economic Development and Cultural Changes 25(3).

Dwyer, Larry and Peter Forsyth Ed. (2006). *International Handbook on the Economics of Tourism,* Edward Elgar, UK.

Fisher, A.C. and J.V. Krutilla, (1972). *Determination of Optimal Capacity of Resource-Based Recreation Facilities.* Natural Resource Journal, Vol. 12, pp. 417-444.

Foster, D. (1985). *Travel and Tourism Management,* Macmillan, London.

Foster, J. (1964). *Sociological Consequences of Tourism,* International Journal of Comparative Sociology, 3(3).

Freeman, A.M. (1979). *The Benefits of Environmental Improvement.* John Hopkins University Press, Baltimore.

Friedman, J. and W. Alonso (1965). *Regional Development and Planning—A Reader*, MIT Press, Cambridge and London.

Gamage, A.R., N. Shaw and R. Ihalanayke, (1997). *The Cost of Political Upheaval to International Tourism in Srilanka.* A Paper Presented to the International Seminar on Tourism and Economic Development, Bhubaneswar, India.

Gearing, C., W. Swart and T. Var (1976). *Planning for Tourism Development—Quantitative Approaches*, Preager Publishers, New York.

Gearing, C.; W. Swart and T. Var (1978). *A Multi-Period Planning Model for Tourism Development*, Proceedings of the Fifth Pacific Regional Science Conference, Simon Frasher University, Vancouver, Canada, June 1978.

Ghali, M.A. (1976). *Tourism and Economic Growth: An Empitical Study*. Economic Development and Cultural Change 24 (3).

Gray, H.P. (1970). *International Travel International Trade*, Lexington, Heath.

Green, H.C. Hunter and B. Moore (1990). *Application of the Delphi Technique in Tourism*, ATR 17 (270-79).

Greenwood, D.J. (1976). *Tourism as an Agent of Change*—A *Spanish Basque Case*, ATR 5 (2).

Hadker, N.; S. Sharma; A. David; T.R. Muraleedharan; S. Geeta and P.G. Balu (1995). *Are People in Developing Countries Willing to Pay for Natural Reserve Preservation*? IGIDR, Mumbai.

Hirschman, A.O. (1958). *Strategy of Economic Development.* Yale University Press, New Haven.

Hotelling, H. (1931). *The Economics of Exhaustible Resource*, Journal of Political Economy 39 (137-75).

Indian Institute of Public Opinion (1978). *Report on Indian Tourism Performance.*

Indian Statistical Institute, Calcutta (1982). *Foreign Tourist Survey.*

Jafari, J. and A. Dean (1988). *Tourism as the Subject of Doctoral Dissertations*, ATR, Vol. 15, pp. 407-29.

James, A.J. and M.N. Murty (1999). *Measuring Non-User Benefits from Cleaning Ganges.* Working Series No. E/202/99, Institute of Economic Growth Delhi.

Jia, L. and C. Tisdell (1993). *Resource Redistribution and Regional Income Inequality in China*, Discussion Paper No. 9318, Deptt. of Economics, University of Otago, Dunedin.

Johnson, R. and D.B. Suits (1983). "A Statistical Analysis of the Demand for Visits to US National Parks—Travel Cost and Seasonality," *Journal of Travel Research,* Vol. 22, pp. 21-24.

Kahn, R.F. (1931). *The Relation of Home Investment to Unemployment Economic Journal 41*(173-198).

Kaul, R.N. (1985). *Dynamics of Tourism—A Trilogy, Sterling,* New Delhi.

Kealy, M.J. and R.C. Bishop (1986). *Theoretical and Empirical Specification Issues in Travel Cost Demand Studies*, American Journal of Agricultural Economics, 68(3).

Keynes, J.M. (1933). *The Multiplier: The New Statesman and Nation*, 1 April, pp. 405-07.

Kottke, M. (1987). *Estimating Economic Impact of Tourism*, ATR 8(3).

Kottlar, P.H. (1967). *Marketing Management Analysis*, Planning, Control, Englewood Cliff, N.J.

Kumar, S.C. (1997). *Performance and Prospects of Tourism Industry in India*, Papers Presented in the 4th International Conference on Development and Future Studies held at Bangi, 2-4 September.

Lanza, A.; Anil Markandya and F. Pigliaru (2005). *The Economics of Tourism and Sustainable Development*, Edward Elgar.

Leontief, W.W. (1956). "Factor Proportion and the Structure of American Trade, Further Theoretical and Empirical Analysis." *Review of Economics and Statistics*, November (386-407).

Lime, D.W. and G.H. Stamkey (1971). "A Selected Bibliography of Literature Related to Recreational Carrying Capacity Decision-Making." *Forest Recreation Symposium*, Suracuse, New York School of Forestry.

Linstone, A.H. and M. Turoff Eds. (1975). *The Delphi Method-Techniques and Applications reading M.A.* Addison Wesley Publishing.

Mallen, B. (1977). "French Canadian Consumer Behaviour-Comparative Lessons from the Published Literature and Private Corporate Marketing Studies." *Advertising and Sales Club of Montreal.*

Mathieson, A. and C. Wall (1982). *Tourism, Economic, Physical and Social Impacts*, Longman.

McConnell, K.E. (1980). *Valuing Congested Recreational Sites, Journal of Environmental Economics and Management*, 7 (389-94).

McDonnell, I. (1996). *The Interfrag Marketing Continuum: A Tool for Tourism Marketers.* A Paper Presented in Asia Pacific Tourism Association, 1996 Conference, Townsville, North Queens land.

Meadows, D.D.; J.R. Meadows and W. Behrens (1972). *The Limit to Growth: A Report on the Predicament of Mankind.* New York, Universe Books.

Medlik, S. and V.T.C. Middleton (1985). *The Tourist Product and its Marketing*, International Tourism Quarterly, February.

Mednick, H.H. (1975). *A Markov Chain Model of Travel Patterns of US Visitors to Ontario*, Journal of Leisure Research, 7(4).

Mihalic, T. (2006). *Nature-based Products, Ecotourism and Adventure Tourism, In Tourism Business Frontiers* (Ed. Buhalis D and C Costa) Elsevier.

Mitra, A. and K. Chattopadhyay (2003). *Environment and Nature-Based Tourism: An Endeavour at Sustainability*. Kanishka, Delhi.

Morey, R.C. and D.A. Dittman (1997). *An Aid in Selecting the Bran, Size and Other Strategic Choices for a Hotel*, Journal of Hospitality and Tourism Research 21(1), 71-99.

Myrdal, G. (1957). *Economic Theory and Underdeveloped Regions*, London.

Myrdal, G. (1972). *Asian Drama—An Enquiry into the Poverty of Nations.*

National Council of Applied Economic Research (1975). *Cost-Benefit Study of Tourism*, New Delhi.

Navarro, P. and A. Spencer (2001). *September 11, 2001, Assessing the Costs of Terrorism*. The Milken Institute Review 4.

Organization of American States (1979). *Information on Document Seminar to Secure a Lasting Tourism*, Washington D C, OAS.

Pearce, D. (1981). *Tourist Development*, Longman, London.

Pigou, A.C. (1920). *Economics of Welfare.*

Pizam, A. (1982). *Tourism and Crime—Is There a Relationship*? JTR 20 (3).

Richardson, S.L. and J. Crompton (1988). *Vacation Pattern of*

French and English Canadians, Annals of Tourism Research ATR, Vol. 15.

Sakai, H.; H. Sakamoto and M. Toida (1983). *Measurement of Economic Impact of Tourism by Input-Output Model: Case Studies of Malaysia*, Singapore and Thailand presented at Workshop on Economic Impact Analysis for Tourism Policy Orientation 22-26 August, Bangkok.

Sau, R. (1993). *Purchasing Power Parity, Unequal Exchange and Foreign Direct Investment*, Economic and Political Weekly, September 11.

Sen, Amartya (1980). *Strategies of Economic Development*, Feasibility Constraints and Planning *In* Resources, Value and Development.

Sen, P. (1985). "Foreign Exchange Earnings and Employment Generation," *The Future of International Tourism with Reference to India, Indian Council of Trade and International Economic Relation*, New Delhi.

Shackle, G.L.S. (1967). *The Years of High Theory and Tradition of Economic Thought, 1926-1939*, Cambridge University Press.

Sharp, H. and P. Mott (1956). *Consumer Decisions in the Metropolitan Family*, Journal of Marketing, 21 October.

Singh, T.V. (1989). *The Kulu Valley, Impact of Tourism Development in the Mountain Areas*, Himalayas Books, New Delhi.

Smith, V.K. and J.V. Krutila (1982). *Towards Reformulation of the Role of Natural Resources in Economic Models, In* Smith-Krutila (Eds.) Exploration in Natural Resources Economics, Baltimore.

Stephen, S. (1997). *Sustainable Development a Paradoxical Paradigm*, Search Bulletin, 12(2) Bangalore.

Strang, W.A. (1970). *Recreation and the Local Economy.* Technical Report No. 4, University of Wisconsin.

Swart W.W.; T. Var and C.E. Gearing (1978). *Operations Research Application to Tourism,* ATR 4(1).

Theuns, H. Leo (1989). *Multidisciplinary Focus on Tourism,* ATR 16 (189-204).

Theuns, H. Leo (2001). *Sustainable Long Haul Tourism: Does it Really Exist?* Tourism Recreational Research, Lucknow, India.

Tisdell, C. (2005). *A Review of Structural Features of International Tourism: Economic Influences and Its Vulnerability, In* Global Review of Economic Research 1(1).

Um, S. and K.L. Crompton (1992). *The Roles of Perceived Inhibitors and Facilitators in Pleasure Travel Destination Decisions,* Journal of Travel Research, Winter 18-25.

Walsh, R.G. and L.O. Gilliam (1982). *Benefits of Wilderness Expansion with Excess Demand for Indian Peaks,* Western Journal of Agricultural Economics, 7 July, 1-12.

Walter, C.K. and H.M. Tong (1977). *A Local Study of Consumer Vacation Travel Decisions,* Journal of Travel Research (JTR) 15(4).

Ward, Barbara and R. Dubos (1972). *Only One Earth—The Care and Maintenance of a Small Planet,* Harmondworth, Middlesex, Penguin Books.

Weightman, B.A. (1987). *Third World Tour Landscape,* ATR 14 (2).

Wen, J. and C. Tisdell (1996). *Spatial Distribution of Tourism in China: Economic and other Influences, In* Tourism Economics Ed. Clem, Tisdell.

Wetzel, J.N. (1977). *Estimating the Benefits of Recreation Under*

Conditions of Congestion, Journal of Environmental Economics, 4 (239-246).

World Commission on Environment and Development (1987). *Our Common Future*, Oxford University Press.

Wright, A.U. (1956). *The Genesis of the Multiplier Theory*, Oxford Economic Papers 8 (181-193).

Zakaria, F. (2001). *The Return of History. In* J. Hoge and G Rosse Eds. *How Did This Happen: Terrorism and the New War* (307-17) New York: Public Affairs.

Zinder, H. (1969). *The Future of Tourism in the Eastern Caribbean*, Washington D.C.

Author Index

Subject Index

SUBJECT INDEX